SOAP BEHIND THE EARS

BOOKS BY
CORNELIA OTIS SKINNER

*

EXCUSE IT, PLEASE!

TINY GARMENTS

DITHERS AND JITTERS

SOAP BEHIND THE EARS

SOAP BEHIND THE EARS

BY CORNELIA OTIS SKINNER

DRAWINGS BY *alajálov*

DODD, MEAD & COMPANY
NEW YORK ✧ 1943

PRINTED IN THE UNITED STATES OF AMERICA
BY THE VAIL-BALLOU PRESS, INC., BINGHAMTON, N. Y.

ACKNOWLEDGMENT

Grateful acknowledgment for permission to reprint these articles is made to *The New Yorker, Theatre Arts Monthly* and *The New York Times*.

CONTENTS

CONTENTS

THE DEFENSE OF LONG ISLAND

THE
DEFENSE OF LONG ISLAND

THERE'S lots going on these days down in our section of Long Island in regard to defense. Just about everyone, with the possible exception of myself, is frantically engaged in an activity they call "doing something" about it. Not that by this confession I mean to cover myself with white feathers. My patriotism is, I trust, as sterling as that of my neighbors but it would seem my usefulness isn't and I've reached the depressing conclusion that in case of invasion the only thing I can do for my country is die.

This was all brought home to me one quiet evening

last month when our local Paul Revere whizzed up to our front door in a car covered with patriotic stickers, mud and, one suspected, foam, handed me a questionnaire and in a voice of splendidly controlled excitement as if the enemy were already at Patchogue, told me to fill it out. I squared my shoulders, tried to look like Molly Pitcher and told him I would. He nodded severely (people in heroic mood apparently don't smile very much, unless it's into the cannon's mouth), made a gesture that was a suppressed salute, spurred his car and sped off into the night. It was all pretty momentous. I felt I ought to go wake my little boy and take down my grandfather's Appomattox gun. Only my little boy wasn't asleep and my grand-father never fought at Appomattox and the only guns handy were a BB and an air-rifle. I hastened inside to the nearest light and unfolded the questionnaire as if it had been a dispatch from General Washington's headquarters. It started out simply enough inquiring the name, age, and nationality of each member of our household. Then it got complicated for after every individual was written "Experience" followed by a large question mark. I presumed this meant of a na-ture that might prove of service to one's country for it seemed hardly probable that in my own case the in-formation "Broadway, summer stock and radio" would qualify me for anything much except a camp-follower. True, during the last war I had done my bit. Twice a week I submitted my little body to the experimental ministrations of the members of my mother's First Aid class who tried out splints, fancy bandages and tourniquets on my childish limbs . . . a treatment which has, I'm certain, had a far-reaching after-effect on my circulation. But I hardly felt such kindergarten training would impress the defense organization, so I left an apologetic blank. When it came to my family, however, I could state with pride that my ten-year-old was a lance-corporal in the Knickerbocker Greys and that my husband was a hero of the bloodless war of the Mexican border and from this grim experience could qualify at killing tarantulas. The maid I wrote off as a "vivandière" and the cook I put down as "cook."

The next page began with a flattering inquiry into the variety and type of motors we were credited with. Aside from the family car, they asked how many and what sort of trucks and tractors did we have. They might as well have asked how many and what sort of locomotives and steam-shovels did we have. When it came to "Boats and Water-Craft" I could answer with a certain degree of satisfaction that we are the happy owners of a duck-boat, a canoe and two air-mattresses which, in the event of evacuating the island, might be pressed into service. Being too much afraid of guns even to count them, I left the reporting of our modest arsenal up to my husband. Under the startling heading of "Fire-Fighting Equipment" I assured them that they could count on us for 5 buckets, 2 Pyrene Extinguishers (small size) and a generous portion of Long Island Sound. There were some further inquiries as to how many sheets and pillow cases we had on hand. At first I took this to mean how many were in a state fit only to be torn into bandages but subsequently learned that at any moment officials from an emergency hospital might descend upon my linen closet and denude it. They then asked what live-stock we had, to which, after some hesitancy I replied "three dogs and a trained paraquet," later eliminating the word "trained" for fear my feathered friend might get drafted into the message-carrying service. There were other odd questions such as had we a gasolene tank and how much could it hold, to which I wanted to answer "only in the car and it's usually empty," but felt this was no time for flippancy; and how many beds could I keep "available," which sounded sassy and a little frightening. The questionnaire ended with "MISC." I didn't quite know what to list here unless maybe "one archery outfit, two pairs of skis, some

Cape Cod burners. Also scythes, pitchforks and the spirit of '76."

A few days later one of our more civic-minded inhabitants came to call. She had an air of having completed her preparedness like someone who, by October, has tied up all her Christmas presents. She opened the interview by telling me that she had "on complete authority" the alarming information that in case of invasion the Army wasn't going to defend Long Island . . . which gives one a faint idea of what the Army thinks of Long Island. An attack on New York would mean the bombing of all bridges and then where would we be? I was about to answer, "Still on Long Island, I guess," when she fixed me with a recruiting-poster stare and asked what I was going to do about it. I said somewhat lamely that since the Army had abandoned us to our fate, it wouldn't do much good for me to take a stand alone. She assured me I'd not be called upon for anything so drastic and went on to ask if I'd ever done any professional nursing, if I could qualify as an automobile mechanic, if I knew anything about electricity or steam-fitting, if I understood Morse. I said no, and I'd never piloted an airplane nor steered a submarine and I was sorry but I didn't know a thing about mine-sweeping. She gave me a look that might have been "FIFTH COL-

-{ 7 }-

UMNIST!!" in neon lights and asked me what, if anything, I could do. For a moment I was tempted to say I could speak French, Italian and German and could dance the Conga, hoping vaguely I might be commandeered into some more glamorous branch of the espionage service; but she wasn't the kind of woman you could swing anything like that with. So I said meekly I didn't know but that though humble I was willing—nay, proud, to do my part. For a time she sat mulling over my shortcomings then finally informed me that in the event of the bombing of the New York bridges I would be expected to take in refugees from Queens. I started to ask her if she couldn't make that refugees from Brooklyn Heights but decided I'd done enough already to set myself up as the community Benedict Arnold. I assured her I'd be ready with open arms to receive the homeless ones from Queens.

Her visit convinced me that as an asset to Uncle Sam I am a complete liability and started me looking about for ways in which to become more useful. It appears there are any number of organizations one can join. The First Aid class meets regularly. They are very industrious and particularly cheerful these days because the encouraging rumor has got about that the army bombers which manoeuvre daily above us, missing the town water-tank by inches, carry a few live bombs and who can tell when one of these high-explosives might fall out? I'd be no good at First Aid. Coming from a long line of people whose hands tremble, it would be nigh to impossible for me to do a neat bandaging job and in times of stress they'd end up in having to bandage me. Then there's a Ladies' Ambulance Corps who put on a pretty impressive act at all out-door events, rushing in formation onto a field and surrounding a prone and willing volunteer whom they pick up and hurtle head-long through the back door of their vehicle in the manner of stoking a bake-oven. This splendid organization I should hesitate to join because I have a feeling they'd always make me play the rôle of the body.

Of course one can go in for special instruction in things. Two of my friends have been putting in some happy grease-filled hours lying under automobiles in various garages while a lady mechanic stands above them and tells them what she thinks they must be looking at. Others commute twice a week to Manhattan to take a course in "canteen work" which, as far as I'm able to fathom, means a course in how to hand out sandwiches. One might, of course, join the dietician group, but from the point of view of military strategy that strikes me as rather superfluous training, because

I've always understood that in times of war you ate what you could get and in case of siege were grateful for a few tasty rats. Perhaps the most colorful corps hereabouts is the Girls' Rifle Team. This is composed of some ten or fifteen middle-aged Annie Oakleys who, girding for parachutists, practice regularly under the terrified tutelage of a state trooper who obviously regards this as one of the major hazards in his line of duty. I declined with polite regrets an invitation to become one of this daring band. I've occasionally taken a crack at rifle-practice but have always had a terrible time trying to aim, pull the trigger and stop up my ears all at once. Besides I feel somehow that death at the hands of a parachutist is less inglorious than as a result of a neighbor's careless aim . . . which might not be so careless at that. Then there are a few enterprising ladies who have gotten together and are taking up in a big way the study of map-reading. They go about with looks of high purpose, compasses and expensive topographical maps which aren't half as nice as the ones Socony or Texaco give you free. The result of their researches seem to be that you may think you know your way from the station to your own front door but you can't be really sure until you've gotten out your compass and taken bearings. Besides any day now they may start changing around the road-signs in order to baffle an invading host. I've always suspected a few of our road-signs anyway of being left-overs from the days when the loyal Long Islanders wanted to put Lord Howe on the wrong track. I don't believe I want to take this course. After ten years I've just about gotten the hang of the roads down here and I don't want to get balled up by trying to be accurate.

An indication that we are not behind in our defense program is the fact that we now have an air-raid warden. He has us all learning how to turn out our lights —a duty which, whenever there's a severe thunderstorm, the Long Island Lighting Company usually relieves us of anyway. Besides occasional evenings spent practicing black-outs *en famille,* we are urged when we can to go in for blind-driving. This ought to prove easy for certain members of the community who every week-end do quite a bit of blind-driving to and from the club and the village roadhouse.

Aside from knitting tiny garments for the Red Cross and giving away almost every cooking utensil we ever owned in the aluminum drive, my contribution to National Defense has been negligible. I have yet to find my niche. I'm apparently one of those unfortunates necessary to times of stress who go down in history as "those who went under." Of course I can always look forward to the visitation of those refugees from Queens but they might decide to migrate Jones Beach way. I guess I'd best resign myself to the idea I mentioned at the start that all I can do is get killed. . . . And that, incidentally, is something which, after the local Minute Men and Women see this article, will probably happen to me anyway.

BICYCLE BUILT
FOR ONE

BICYCLE BUILT FOR ONE

FASHIONS in sport seem to change as rapidly as fashions in hair-do's. No sooner do we accustom ourselves to the sight of women with childish shoulder-length manes looking (some of them) like aging Little Evas, than Antoine decrees we must get used to them looking as if they'd just emerged from the tub. And no sooner have we at considerable expenditure equipped ourselves with Alpine outfits and acclimated ourselves to the borax-laden air of department-store ski-slides than someone (doubtless Mr. Spaulding with encouragement from Mr. Abercrombie and Mr. Fitch) announce that the runner must make way for the wheel and that bicycles are now *de rigueur*. And as I understand the term, *de rigueur* is a pat one, especially when followed by *mortis*. I dare say next year someone will come across an old diabolo set and we'll all be trying to remember how the devil we used to play that. For one of the most trying aspects of these shifting fads in sport is having to reconstruct them from childhood days only to discover one must also reconstruct one's self. At least this one must. As a girl I was the Sonja Henie of my block . . . only in those far-off days it wasn't Sonja Henie but a fairy-tale creature with a Godiva swash of blond hair and the more pronounceable name of Charlotte, accent on the *lotte* (which I guess dates me alright). Roller-skating became smart a few years ago and with confidence and a new pair of skates I joined the happy throng in the Central Park Mall, only to find that what I resembled was neither Henie nor Charlotte but a performing bear, only the bear would have done a good deal better.

Time was when I played a reasonably good game of croquet but Alexander Woollcott put me off his court and told me never to try again, and although in my salad days I swatted a neat ping-pong ball, in my present days, which might I suppose, be termed dessert and nuts, it looks as if I couldn't even swat a fly.

I have been on the point of retiring myself like Man-
o'-War and leaving the field of sport to suppler and
more youthful enthusiasts. Now, however, comes the
craze for cycling to renew my faith in my muscles
—or rather to create the hallucination that I still
have some. I have apparently not forgotten how to
balance and pedal. This I proved to myself a season
ago in Bermuda where, primed with ambition and one
too many green swizzles, I rode so long and so violently the first day, I developed an unfortunate and
painful variety of saddle-sore which lasted for the
duration of my sojourn on that happy island. What
though sore and spavined, I at least was reassured that
here was one form of youthful activity I could still
execute and when I got home I bought a bicycle. That
is, I left the purchasing of it to a friend who assured
me he would get me one cheap. He got me a cheap
one all right. A rattly contraption of tin and wire, it
looks as if it would collapse under the weight of anyone other than a child of three. The only reason it
doesn't is that the wire and tin are supported by a
cast-iron structure so heavy and awkward, riding the
thing is like peddling along on a Victorian funeral
bench. With parsimonious optimism I consoled myself with the thought that this would merely make
exercise the more strenuous and if cycling were

good for the figure, let Carole Lombard look to her laurels and limbs.

After all these years I may have kept the ability to keep my balance. What I can't seem to keep is my breath. One lap around my driveway . . . a very abbreviated driveway and as flat as Kansas . . . reduces me to the condition of a six-day bike racer on the last sprint of the sixth day. I thought at first the brake must be jammed in some way and tested that mechanism to find out whether or not it took hold. It did. Immediately. In fact, so completely was the hold it took, it caused me to lose mine and catapult onto the handle-bars. Only the fact that by then the front wheel was safely imbedded in the hedge prevented a complete somersault. There's no midway concession about my brakes. Either you're going full speed ahead or you're stopped dead still and it's a nice problem in acrobatic technique to determine the exact movement in which to jump. "Full speed ahead" be it understood, is merely a conventional phrase that can apply only to those rare and happy moments when I'm going down-hill. The rest of the time any forward progress is effected in a labored and serpentine manner that wears the agonizing aspect of a nightmare victim trying to avoid an onrushing locomotive. This motion occurs not only going up-hill,

but on the flat as well. I'm afraid the explanation lies
not in the inadequate frame of my machine but in the
more than adequate frame of my person. I may as
well face the fact that I'm no longer the brown slip of
a thing whose pet form of exhibitionism was to skim
down the steepest hill in town with my feet on the
handle-bars and my arms folded Cossack-wise. Nor
does it seem possible that I was ever the debonair little
hoyden who one Sunday evening on a double dare
rode down the steps of the school verandah and ended
in the outraged stomach of a visiting divine who had
come to talk to us in Chapel about Love and Toler-
ance. These bright pictures recur to me as I weave
jerkily along the road, the easy prey of every passing
car, for every now and then, as if prompted by a
subconscious suicidal mania, I swerve about in a sudden circle which surprises and frightens me quite
badly. Mine seems to be the technique of the vaude-
ville cyclist confined to the space of a night-club
dance-floor. All of which adds the stimulus of danger
to the sport.

One thing I'd forgotten about this beloved old
pastime is the number of things that hurt. Strange
that with the advance of science in the way of painless
dentistry and the like they haven't invented painless
pedals. These hellish contraptions haven't in the least

improved since the days of my childhood when, goaded by rage and pain, I used to pick up a stick and beat my old bike into what I hoped was insensibility. The pedals of to-day pinch and cut as much as ever and my ankles are again in a state of minced beef. Then there's seat trouble. I don't know whether this originates in the bicycle's seat or in mine, but the result ends definitely in the latter and for the first time in a hitherto callous life due to an anatomy not so callous, my heart goes out in sympathy to the horse that has become galled. Maybe there are more uncomfortable seats on things like McCormick reapers or flag-poles, but I doubt it.

On par with the physical distress is the moral. I've about decided that the chief benefit derived from my bicycling is the diversion it makes for others. I recently overheard my son asking his next-door pal if he'd come over, offering as an inducement the irresistible bid that he'd "get my mother to ride her bike for us," as against the latter's less tantalizing bid of having just acquired a new batch of funnies. It seems it doesn't necessarily require a red wig and false feet in order to put on a good clown act.

Incidentally, if you know of anybody who'd be interested, I have a lady's bicycle for sale. Practically new and awfully good exercise. Also if any of you know Carole Lombard, you might pass along the word that she has nothing to fear . . . at least not for the time being.

REMORSE BY
THE SEA

REMORSE BY THE SEA

(A silent soliloquy)

MY the sun feels good. Just what I needed. I'm glad I got up after all. It isn't half as bad as I thought it would be. The sun will soon cure me. Not that there's anything to cure. Just a touch of neuritis, plus that red wine.

That's all this is. Just a touch of neuritis. My goodness, I've had that when I haven't had a drop. . . . I mean the sun certainly feels good.

Darn bright, though. These glasses aren't any good. What one really needs is blinkers . . . *are* blinkers . . . or a black bandage might be handy.

-{ 25 }-

This settles it! I'm never going to take another drink. Never! Not that I took too much last night. I mean I wasn't really what you'd call . . . I was just a little elated. Elated. That's what it was. Because I didn't do a thing I shouldn't have. Except maybe that time I went out and sat . . . Who was that man anyway?

It was that red wine. I ought to remember you can't mix red wine with anything because, after all, I didn't have much to drink. Just those two old-fashioneds at the Browns' (you couldn't count the dividend, it was mostly water). Then just one more cocktail before dinner at the Joneses'. Why on earth do the Joneses serve only stingers? And in those enormous glasses! Really very bad taste.

Wish I hadn't thought of bad taste.

There's that good-looking Turner man. He never drinks. That's the way to be. He has just as good a time. Better. I don't enjoy myself a bit when I'm . . . But I wasn't really. I mean I behaved perfectly. I remember with clarity everything I did. I remember trying to do the Suzie Cue which was perhaps a little informal of me. And then wasn't there a moment when I was crying? I have a dim recollection of crying. Crying quite bitterly and hopelessly. What was that about? Oh, dear.

And who was that man I sat out in the . . . Not that it matters. By that I mean to say not that anything occurred. Still, it's annoying not to remember. Like trying to think of a title of a book. How degrading not to remember. I'll never take another drink. You can have every bit as good a time on Coca-Cola. Look at that nice Turner fellow. Better not look at him, though. He might come over and talk and I haven't the strength. Besides, I'm not looking my best. My eyes are rather bloodshot. That's, of course, from crying that time.

Wish I could remember what made me cry. . . . No, I'll never touch a drop from now on. Just sherry and a little wine (red wine's all right if you don't mix the grain and the grape). Now and then a glass of champagne. Wonder if a champagne cocktail mightn't be a good restorative? After all people drink them at sea for mal-de-mer. Even respectable old dowagers.

Oh, my head! Nothing worse than neuritis. Or maybe I'm coming down with elephantiasis.

I'm certain nobody last night thought I was at all— I mean they were pretty well oiled themselves. I behaved with perfect decorum. I admit my imitation of Shirley Temple didn't get over very big and then there was that episode in the car. Or was it an episode and who was that man anyway?

I am in great pain. Oh, very great pain. I don't re-member ever having been in such pain before. Even when I was in the perils of child-birth. Of course I had an anaesthetic then. I wonder if it would be pos-sible to get an anaesthetic now? Why don't I drive over to the hospital and say I've come for an anaes-thetic? Only my breath might give me away. In fact it might anaesthetize the anaesthetist. How vile! How vile and unwomanly!

I wonder if a swim would help. A fine rugged plunge into the clean, cool brine. Better not. A cloud of steam would probably rise in my wake . . . like a hot horse-shoe in whatever they plunge a hot horse-shoe into.

Why should I feel sick? Must be that fish. That's what it is. Fish. Still, it tasted all right and I took some brandy . . . two or three glasses, in fact. And they say brandy settles fish. Maybe that's what settled me. Ha-Ha-Ha! Joke!

Wonder if a little brandy mightn't. No. Definitely no. No more hard liquors. Imagine a woman of my re-finement even thinking about hard liquor, let alone indulging in it.

Must that little girl make so darn much noise tramping about in the sand? And her mother! Just look at her! Smug type. Probably got up early and went to church. I couldn't stand church today. The sound of the quarters dropping into the plate would just about kill me.

The sun really is curing me. I'm beginning to feel fine.

The Hell I am!

More unnecessary noises in this place. That woodpecker, for instance. Why should he come crashing around this morning of all mornings? What could be worse? I know what *could* be worse. To be a woodpecker on a morning like this. Ooooh! I wish I hadn't thought of that.

Wish I hadn't drunk that red wine.

Wish I hadn't. . . . Just what did happen in that car?

Maybe what I need is one tiny wee little dose of Scotch. Purely medicinal, mind you. Hair of the dog idea. I won't like it, of course. Still, it might be just the thing to bring me round.

There are the Smiths. I guess they're feeling pretty awful, too. Maybe they'd like a little dose, too. I might ask them to drop by the house for one quick one. Of course I won't take anything except . . .

I wonder if there are any lemons in the house? Whiskey sours might be nice. . . . For the Smiths, I mean. I won't have any. Although a whiskey sour sounds like the only thing I could face.

If I ask the Smiths I ought to ask Mabel and Sam over, too. And then it might be polite to tell Harriet to bring over her house-guest. And the Turner fellow might like to come over for a tomato-juice cocktail. I'll have one with him. Prove to myself and the world you can do just as well on tomato-juice. Good clean tomato-juice.

As a matter of fact tomato-juice isn't very good for me. It gives me a sort of rash. I'm sure this morning it would give me hives. No, it would be wiser not to take tomato-juice after all.

Still, I'll have to take something. And I really need something to bring me round. How degrading.

I'm perfectly certain if it hadn't been for that red wine, I'd be feeling fine. Because cocktails alone don't hurt me. Don't hurt me at all. The thing to do is to stick to one kind of drink and then you're all right. That's the thing to do. That would be the thing to do today. If I don't take any red wine, I mean.

I guess I'll have old-fashioneds. . . . For the crowd, I mean. Maybe I'll take just one instead of that dose of Scotch. That'll clear my head. Then maybe I'll be able to remember who that man was. Maybe he'll turn out to be one of the people I've asked. In which case I'll have to take a second old-fashioned. Well, that won't hurt as long as I don't take any red wine afterwards.

It was that red wine. That's what it was. Hereafter I'll never touch another drop.

Of red wine.

THE VOLGA
TONGUE

THE VOLGA TONGUE

IN view of the recent findings of the Dies Committee, I feel it's about time I came clean and confessed that I am studying Russian. Sooner or later some old federal snoop is going to catch me poring over a Russian book which for all he knows may be a manual on how to introduce Marx into the nation's kindergartens and is going to report me to Washington. Not that any girl wouldn't be delighted to be regarded as a potential Mata Hari. But it would be such a come-down for everybody when the tell-tale tract turned out to be a conversational text-book and the page over which I was caught red-handed . . . or in the case of Russian print, red-eyed . . . a subversive little treatise on how to order a meal . . . and a pretty terrible meal at that. Moreover the F.B.I. inquisitors would ask me what everybody else does when I tell them I'm studying Russian . . . "Why?" The answer to this is "Because I've always had a hankering to be able to speak a little Russian" and again they say "Why?" and I don't for the life of me know. I have no remote desire ever to visit the U.S.S.R. nor do I give a hoot about reading Pushkin in the original. I don't even want to make a hit with Serge Obolensky. I merely want to acquire what is known as a smattering of the language. (At that point my typewriter which sometimes acts more like a ouija-board wrote "stammering" instead of "smattering" and I guess it has the right idea.) I don't see why I'm any more eccentric than tired business men who start in to learn the rhumba or those jaded women who begin "taking up" things like Yoga or the accordion.

I started in by taking a few private lessons from a governess who, if one was to believe her, had taught everybody from the last Empress to Ivan the Terrible. Her circumstances were decidedly reduced and so, I discovered, was any ability she might once have had for teaching. My cook, to whom the sight of a thin person is a disgrace to the house, used to send her in little snacks and I made the mistake of allowing it. Russian is difficult enough to make out when pronounced with perfect clarity and when heard through a mist of coffee and cake it's nigh to impossible. She spent most of her time regaling me with stories of her better days. How she used to play croquet with the Gallitzins and lotto with the Romanoffs and how every Easter her dear patron, a Count and Countess Something-sky would shower her with beautiful jewel-encrusted golden eggs, which, for a working-girl, must have come in handy. She was one of those Slavs with tragic eyes which they make up to look even more tragic . . . in fact they look as if someone had pasted them the night before. She was always "tarribly, tarribly deprassed" and I guess my stabs at pronouncing her mother tongue didn't do much to disperse the gloom. We struggled somewhat mournfully through the alphabet and I managed to memorize an embarrassing little song about a boy named Igor who keeps asking his father to bring him a red cap from the fair, which no one ever seems interested in hearing me sing. Then I was informed that the woman was an impostor . . . she had never played lotto with the Romanoffs she hadn't even played Old Maid with Rasputin, nor was she really Russian. She was Latvian. I had no idea what being Latvian meant and still haven't but it was a good excuse for letting her go. I decided to strike out for myself.

I learned to read the stuff after a limping fashion. It's not as difficult to decipher as I'd like those whom I try to impress to think. All one has to do is to learn a completely new alphabet and remember that nothing is ever the way it looks. For instance "PECTOPAH" is "RESTAURANT," "HET" is "NIETT" and means "NO," while "B" means "IN" and is pronounced like the beginning of a stifled yawn. Primed with this knowledge and a beginner's optimism, I purchased a set of those language gramophone records with accompanying text-books by means of which, in some thirty lessons, one is supposed to become verbally equipped to engage rooms at a hotel, call on a Grandmother, get a shave (I'm glad of this) and tell a mechanic what's wrong with your radio. The recordings have been made by gentlemen with deep voices worthy the Moscow Art Theatre. They utter everyday phrases and sentences and carry on supposedly simple conversations with each other. The books furnish the text, translation and grammar and the records do the rest. You play them over and over, setting the needle back whenever you don't quite gather what's being said (which is practically constantly) and at the same time you follow along with the text-books . . .

that is, if you're abnormally bright. The theory being that after listening to sufficient repetition of a language one learns to speak it in the instinctive fashion of a little child. Words and phrases caught in the subconscious ring in the head like strains of familiar music and before you know it you're jabbering away as fluently as any waiter. It's a good method and it works fairly well. Only I haven't advanced very far and my subconscious proves to be of the most impractical variety for the words and phrases that keep popping up at the back of what I fatuously call my brain seem all to be completely unessential. For instance, the word for "mustard-pot" a lovely sound . . . "gorchichnitsa" like a star of the Ballet Russe, I never forget, although "fork" and "spoon" elude me. "Feather bed" I could tell you in a second but I can't ever remember "bed" or what goes on it with the possible exception of "person."

My family who are curiously indifferent to my intellectual development do little to encourage me. Loath to forego their favorite radio programs, they object to my use of the living-room machine so I have had to purchase a small portable gramophone that can be carried about with me to such havens for study as out onto the back porch or beside the bath-tub. When I travel, I carry it with me and play the records in the seclusion of my hotel room. Just what the local chambermaid thinks when she sees a respectable-looking woman (at least such is my reluctant belief) enter a room supposedly alone and then some minutes later hears floating out over the transom a low and un-intelligible murmur of masculine voices . . . well, what she thinks isn't hard to guess. Sometimes, no doubt, she informs the house detective who tiptoes up and listens for a while; but upon failure to hear the clink of glasses or the strains of *The Old Mill-Stream* goes away in bewilderment and disgust.

Three text-books go with the course. The first is a sort of prompt-script in Russian of the little dramas that are being enacted on the discs. The next is a literal translation, nostalgically reminiscent of my old Horace trot and the third is a little treatise on the grammar and construction which I glanced at and tossed laughingly over my head. To assist the eye as well as the ear, the first of these volumes is embellished with a series of line drawings illustrating the various goings-on in each lesson. Judging by the styles of the women's garments these were done in the late 1920's and thanks to them I shall always think of a "mother" as a creature with shockingly short skirts and a boyish bob and an "aunt" a horror in a mushroom hat and a waist-line around her knees.

Because of the gradual progress in grammar and vocabulary one has to take each lesson as it comes, regardless of whether or not the subject is of the slightest interest. The series begins with "The Family." This is

a little slice of domestic life or a quiet evening on the Steppes. The illustration shows a living-room that might have stepped straight out of the Bronx. In it is assembled the Family, composed of the Grandfather who smokes a pipe, The Grandmother who reads a book, The Mother who plays a piano . . . an upright, too . . . The Little Girl who sings a song, the Father

who is writing a letter, or trying to; the Son (pronounced "Sin") who is playing a drum; the Little Boy
who throws a ball, just missing the chandelier, and the
Baby who appears to be pulling the tail off the Cat.
The Dog does tricks in a corner and the Maid is carry-
ing out some dishes, although what a lot of dishes are
doing in the living-room it doesn't say. As if this
weren't already a frightening enough prospect of bad
housing, the second lesson shows us the arrival of
guests. To make matters more awful, they turn out to
be the Aunt and Uncle, the Male Cousin and the Female Cousin . . . also known as Niece and Nephew.
They're all terribly glad to see one another and express
their pleasure in hearty greetings such as "How do you
do?" and even "How dost thou do?" which sometimes
becomes "How gets along thy life?" It's a heartwarm-
ing scene and from it one gathers that family life flows
along under the shadow of Lenin just as drearily as it
does under the "L." In the third lesson we look in on
the nursery where three happy children are playing
with the beautiful toys their loving and happy parents
have given them. They are all busy and happy. Even
the cat is happy because Vera (the eldest and happiest)
is giving it milk. A young and dashing nurse is carry-
ing in the baby and they're happy, too; the baby because it belongs to such a happy family and the nurse

we aren't told why, but from the looks of her she probably has a heavy date for later in the evening with a handsome and lascivious Cossack. Half of each lesson is taken up by the "razgovor" . . . ("conversation" to you) of two speakers both male, and both very *basso profundo,* one of whom asks a question which the other answers. The finale to this particular assignment is pretty surprising for after inquiring how old each of the children is and receiving the varied information, the interlocutor says, "How old are you?" and a voice like a Tartar version of Wallace Beery replies, "I am nine years old."

The drawing-room comes next. It looks a good deal like a display window at Ludwig Baumann's and nothing much is happening in it, but there's lots doing in the dining-room. Here in front of a background of tapestry, hunting-trophies and a sideboard that might have been salvaged from an old Fred Harvey restaurant, Mr. and Mrs. Pavloff are throwing a select dinner party. Their guests are Mr. Antonoff and Mr. Grineiff. The host and hostess are sitting side by side after the fashion of the eminent married couples in the early days of Hollywood's élite and a pretty picture it is. One likes to think that under cover of the table Mr. Pavloff is giving Mrs. Pavloff's hand an occasional little squeeze. The guests are distributed on either side of the loving pair. They are all quite dressy, the men in dinner jackets and Mrs. Pavloff in a tasty spangled number like something the Dolly Sisters might have worn. The only amenity that appears at all to be lacking is food. They seem to be dining chiefly on salt, pepper, mustard and olive oil, with the exception of the hostess, who is the fortunate recipient of a plate of soup, which, incidentally, is one of the few Russian words that is comparatively easy to learn. In their lettering it may look like something over a New Haven frat house, but in Russian "soup," believe it or not, is "soup" (pronounced "soup").

From the dining-room one progresses, with discretion, to the bedroom, where a lady (presumably Mrs. Pavloff) is sitting at a dressing-table smiling into a mirror from which her own reflection smiles back at her. A maid stands beside her holding a towel and smiling. The only person who isn't smiling is an individual in a four-poster bed who, in spite of the lights all being on, is sound asleep. His identity is never revealed, which may account for Mrs. Pavloff's smile. It isn't Mr. Pavloff nor is it Mr. Antonoff. Upon closer inspection it looks to be an overgrown glandular child. The subjects one takes up are varied. We spend a pleasant day in the suburbs visiting a friend whose modest house boasts of everything from a conservatory to an old-fashioned hat-rack and a gong (pronounced "gonk"). There is a shopping expedition, a trip to a restaurant and an automobile outing during which a chauffeur asks quite testily, "Surely you can't expect me to examine the sparking plugs!" which, as far as I have been able to find, is the one revolutionary note in the course. One learns what to say to the tobacconist, the barber and the doctor. In the case of the latter the following sentence is not only useful but felicitous: "Doctor, my stomach is playing tricks upon me."

I have struggled along as far as the lesson entitled "Games and Sports." Being allergic to all forms of exercise, I doubt if I shall have much occasion to use the terms and phrases it affords. However, it's a color-ful assignment and very illuminating. One learns that in Russia they play a good deal of "lapta" and they're very keen about "skittles." They also go in for football (pronouncing it to rhyme with "fruit-bowl") and they hold splendid affairs known as "Spartakiads" where youths and gymnasts compete at running, the throwing of the javelin, and the overcoming of ob-stacles (whatever they consist of). They also swim and play chess. The latter is in all seriousness included among their more popular athletics. I may not get much chance to discuss lapta and skittles but there is one sentence for which I am eternally grateful and I can't wait to meet a Russian out socially and suddenly spring it on him. Wouldn't he be surprised if sitting next him at some swank dinner I were to turn to him and say. "I do not shoot bears, but it has happened that I have shot elks." That alone would be worth my months of struggle and the price of the course.

I imagine conversational handbooks have always, in their choice of material, had their quaint side. Not long ago someone showed me a language guide printed in the 18th Century for the benefit of Englishmen who were venturesome enough to travel in the Balkans.

Among the first sentences so indispensable for the traveler that it's printed in three or four different tongues is "Halt! My postilion has just been struck by lightning." At that it doesn't seem any more farfetched than my having shot elks.

NUIT DE SIN

NUIT DE SIN

MONOLOGUE OF A YOUNG MAN BUYING PERFUME

He approaches the counter with caution.
Er . . .
*He stands for a moment dejectedly surveying the
array of bottles as if they were musical glasses and
somebody had commanded him to perform on them.
He looks at the saleslady.*
Er . . .
*She doesn't seem to care. Nobody seems to care. He
clears his throat more loudly than he means to. A saleslady approaches. His spirits revive tremulously.*
Er . . . yes. Have you any perfume . . . ah, that is
any good perfume . . . I mean what makes have
you? Yes, it's for a present. I thought I'd . . . just

what would make a good present for a good . . .
present? *The saleslady suggests a few names. He
smiles apologetically.*
I don't speak . . . ha . . . French . . . ha . . . very
well. What was that? "Parfum pour Blondes?" Well,
no, I don't think that'll do; she's not exactly a blonde
. . . she's sort of . . . sort of . . . ha . . . brindle
. . . I mean. What're some other brands?
The girl asks if he wants something in a bouquet.
Oh, no. Just in a bottle.
*The lady holds out a bottle. He takes it as if it might
suddenly go off.*
Yes, that's a pretty bottle . . . that . . . that certainly
is a pretty bottle, all right. "Amour, Amour." Well,
that might seem a little premature. I mean, up to
now we've just . . .
*The lady has produced another bottle which she
thrusts under his nose. This frightens him quite badly
and he recoils. Then he realizes she's not attacking
him so he smiles awkwardly and sniffs with the
courage of one taking chloroform.*
My! *The girl keeps the bottle under his nose.
That's* fine.
*He sniffs again and wonders how long she's going
to hold it there.*
Yes, that's fine. I guess that's the real thing.

-{ 50 }-

She withdraws the bottle and he feels to make sure his nose is still there.

What's that one? "My Sin?" Your sin, did you say? . . . Oh . . . ha . . . I beg your pardon. What I meant to say was how much is the Sin . . . er I mean her sin . . . This Sin?

The young lady states the price. Pause.

I see. Well . . . I guess that must be good all right.

Pause. She gets out another "flacon" and holds it under his nose. This time he leans forward to sniff it and hits his nose against the saleslady's hand.

I beg your pardon. What's that one? . . . "Evening in Paris?" Say, that's pretty good, isn't it? I was only over there for a short . . . I mean, I don't remember Paris smelling like that . . . How much is an Evening in . . . I mean how much?

Pause.

I see. Haven't you any of those pre-war kinds . . . you know those . . . well . . . ha . . . ha . . . you know, Lemon Verbena. Seems to me I used to hear an aunt of mine talking a lot about Lemon Verbena . . . she seems to think that was great stuff. Even I can tell a smell like Lemon Verbena.

Silently the lady walks to the cheaper end of the counter and returns with a bottle of toilet water which she places scornfully beside the more exotic array.

Oh. Well, I guess my aunt was sort of conservative.

He tries without success to laugh it off. Something in the case attracts his gaze.

Is that a good one? That one.

He tries to point but his finger comes abruptly in contact with the glass, which surprises him a good deal.

No . . . to the left . . . my left. I mean your right . . . No not that one . . . back a little . . . No it isn't that one either. It's . . . well, yes, that's the one.

It isn't, but the girl has brought out five bottles already and he thinks he'd better let it go at that. She holds this again under his nose.

Ha! My nose has gotten sort of deaf. I can't tell one from the other.

He turns slightly and realizes there are several impatient customers waiting silently behind him.

Well now, I'd better make up my mind, hadn't I? Which would you choose . . . if you were a girl which would you choose? I mean if you were my girl . . . I beg your pardon . . . well, supposing somebody said to you, "Choose!" Which would you choose? "N'aimez que moi" or "Indiscreet?"

He feels the women behind him are listening. They are. It is with the utmost will-power he can bring himself to pronounce these names.

The saleslady says, "I can't say, sir. They're all very

fine odeurs."
Yes, but just which odeur . . .
He decides to plunge.
I'll take that one.
He points resolutely between two bottles. The sales-girl picks up one and asks, "This?"
Yes.
She picks up another and says, "Or this?"
Yes, that's it. No, don't send it. I'll deliver it myself. I'll just . . . carry it on my hip . . . I mean I'll take it in my . . . That's fine. Well, I'm very glad I'm sure.
He turns around and bumps into one of the waiting women.
I beg your pardon.
He bumps into another and grazes another on the way out but exits whistling.

THE BODY
BEAUTIFUL

THE BODY BEAUTIFUL

AT least three times a year the average woman tries on dresses in a shop. She finds herself standing before one of those fitting-room mirrors with movable side-panels suggestive of a primitive triptych . . . that is, if she has sufficient imagination to turn the triple reflection of herself in a pink slip into a trio of medieval saints. Such mirrors afford one a lot of seldom beheld angles of one's self and the sudden sight of them comes in the nature of a shock. You find you're staring at yourself rather than at the clothes you're buying; at your profile which somehow isn't at all the way you'd remembered it; at that curious three-quarter view when your face appears to be the shape of a Jordan almond, and at that alarming, almost indecent exposure of the back of your neck. When, furthermore, your eye travels earthward from the nape and is suddenly arrested, not without horror, by the reflection of that portion of the anatomy of which you catch a good glimpse only on these sartorial occasions, and which since the last shopping trip appears to have taken on distressing prominence, you reach the grim conclusion that it's almost too late for clothes to matter.

A recently beheld panorama of myself in the clear, cold light of Bloomingdale's most relentless mirror filled me with such panic, I felt I must do something immediately. Recalling the ads of those numerous "slimming salons" which assure you that within a few weeks and for a price unnamed they can change you from a model for Helen Hokinson into a stand-in for Katherine Hepburn, I decided to take my troubles and my protuberances to one of them. Ever since the days of boarding-school, when I used to send for every free sample from henna rinses to stove-polish, I have always fallen for ads. The sweetheart of J. Walter Thompson, I have a peasant-like belief in whatever miracle they profess to effect.

I made inquiries among my better-shaped ac-quaintances and was told that an establishment in the East Fifties was among the best. The place, though small, was impressive. The façade was what is known as "moderne." Instead of the usual show window, it had sort of port-holes in which terra-cotta dryads (they might even have been hamadry-ads) danced amid bottles of perfume. On the ground floor was a sales and reception room where were displayed cosmetics, evening bags and (although a blizzard was raging outside) dark glasses and sun-tan oil. The place, decorated in Louis something style, had such an air of luxe and "parfum" about it you felt that, instead of streamlining you, they ought to turn you out looking like a Boucher. (Why didn't I live at that time, anyway?) A marquise disguised as a saleswoman was sitting behind the sort of table at which de Sévigné must have written her letters. It now held an enormous appointment book, some atomizer bottles and a very pure white phone. She asked if there were anything she could do for me and I said, "Yes. Reduce my rear," which shocked her very much; but, being of the aristocracy, she managed to smile politely. "Have you made an appointment for a consultation with Mme. Alberta?" "Mme. Alberta?" I echoed. "I'm afraid I haven't heard about her." From the expression of the marquise I might have said I hadn't heard about the Duchess of Windsor.

"I don't think I need any consultation," I said. "I just want to reduce my . . ." her eyebrows flickered ever so slightly and I ended lamely, "I just want to lose a few inches."

"All our clients have a consultation first with Mme. Alberta," was her reply. "She happens to be disengaged at the moment. If you'll please go upstairs I'll phone her you're coming." I climbed a mauve-carpeted stair, wondering what sort of consultation lay in store for me. Would Mme. Alberta greet me with a stethescope or would she be discovered gazing into a crystal? A pretty woman, youngish and frighteningly smart was seated at another period table. I gathered she was Mme. Alberta for she said "How do you do?" She had a very strenuous smile and her accent was so determined to be English it broadened every "a" . . . even in the case of such words as *hand* and *ankle*. It was hard to know how to address her. "Mme. Alberta" sounded embarrassing. She didn't look much like an

Alberta and to call her plain *Madam* was unthink-
able. She was one of those women who are so well-
groomed they are positively "soignée" . . . In their
immaculate presence you feel as if you had several
runs in your stockings. She motioned me to a chair
and listened to the story of my proportions as if it
were a case history. She then quoted me prices and
after accepting my check took out a card resembling
a hospital chart. On it she wrote my name and address and some things that struck me as being singu-
larly irrelevant in the matter of hip reduction . . .
when my child was born, what sicknesses I'd ever
had, the current lie about my age, and my blood-
pressure which, like my Social Security number, is
something I can never remember.

"Now, then, we'll see about your weight."

"I know what I weigh," I said, and added reck-
lessly, "and I don't care. All I'm after is to reduce
my . . ."

"Weight and measurements must be taken every
treatment." Her tone, though polite, implied she
didn't think I was quite bright. "There's the dressing
room. Will you disrobe kindly?" I went to what
seemed to be a daintily furnished sentry box and
disrobed kindly. I felt somehow I was up for a
woman's branch of the Army. A trim mulatto

brought me a sheet and a pair of paper slippers that were the shape and texture of peanut bags. I tried to drape the sheet so I'd look like a Tanagra figure but it wouldn't work, so I arranged it along the more simple lines of a Navajo blanket and emerged with caution. Mme. Alberta, who was waiting, told me to "come this way" and I followed her down a corridor, not without a vague apprehension that at the finish of the trip I might find myself confronted by an anaesthetist. She led me behind a screen, whisked off my sheet in the manner of a mayor unveiling a statue and placed me on a scale, naked as Lot's wife . . . nakeder, because that lady could at least boast of a good coating of salt.

"But I tell you, I *know* what I weigh," I protested weakly and told her. She shed on me the indulgent smile a night nurse might give a psychopathic patient, took my weight which turned out to be exactly what I'd said and then told *me*. "Now for those measurements," she said. "Miss Jones, will you please come here?" Miss Jones proved to be a lovely young thing in a wisp of sky blue tunic. She was of such bodily perfection one had the suspicion that "Miss Jones" was incognito for "Miss America." We were formally introduced . . . Miss Jones in her bright blue suit, I in my bright pink skin. She handed

Mme. Alberta a tape measure in exchange for which Mme. Alberta gave her a pencil and my hospital chart.

"Please mark as I call them, Miss Jones," and as if she hadn't already sufficiently humiliated me, Mme. Alberta began calling out my measurements to the world at large. She measured everything. She even measured my neck, my ankle and the length of my arm. I began to wonder if a suit of acrobat fleshings were thrown in with the course.

"I hardly think you need go to all that trouble," I interposed. "It's just my . . .

"We take all measurements," Mme. Alberta said somewhat acidly and continued to encompass me with the tape measure which was a flexible metal affair . . . very cold and with a tendency to tickle. She accompanied her work with a flow of exclamations that might be taken any way. "Well, *well!*" she'd murmur, or "I *thought* so!" and at times shook her pretty head and went "Tsk! Tsk!"

Having completed her survey, she turned me over to Miss Jones, who had me don a baggy little lemon colored suit . . . the sort of thing that in my girlhood was known as an Annette Kellerman. It contrasted cruelly with her own trim tunic, and I felt more humble than I had in my recent nakedness.

She led the way to an exercise room that contained a mat, a gramophone and far too many mirrors, ordered me onto the mat and proceeded to put me through twenty minutes of hard labor. I rolled and thumped. I stretched and kicked. I jumped and pranced. I also puffed and panted. I stood on my shoulders with my feet in the air; that is, Miss Jones hoisted my feet into the air while I rose up onto a fast-breaking neck and screamed. She never paused to allow me to catch a breath which by now was of such weakened quality it hardly seemed worth while trying to catch it. I tried to take time out . . . to divert her with harmless chatter. But Miss Jones is very strict. Now and then when total collapse seemed imminent, using the therapy of the brass band spurring on exhausted troops, she'd play a lively record on the gramophone calling out "one *and* two *and* three *and* four" as if it were a battle cry. She herself was tireless. She'd do awful things such as picking up her ankle with one hand and holding her foot above her head like a semaphore, and expected me to do likewise. I'm one of those rigid types who, since early childhood, has never been able to lean over and touch my toes—not that I've ever wanted to especially. Moreover, I not only can't raise my foot above my head, I can't even bend far enough to get my hand anywhere near my ankle. Miss Jones tells me I'm seriously hamstrung . . . a nasty expression that makes me feel they've been keeping me in the smoke-house all these years.

It's hard to feel cozy with Miss Jones. She is not only strict, she's exceptionally refined. What I call "middle" she calls *diaphragm,* what I call *stomach* with her goes whimsey and becomes *tummy,* and what I call something else she refers with averted eyes to as *derrière.*

The time dragged almost as heavily as my limbs. Finally Miss Jones said I was a good girl and had done enough for the day (the dear Lord knows the day had done enough for me!) and I might go have my massage. I staggered out and into the capable arms of a Miss Svenson who looked like Flagstad dressed up as a nurse. She took me into a small room, flung me onto a hard table and for forty-five minutes went to work on me as if I were material for a taffy-pulling contest. She kneaded me, she rolled me with a hot rolling pin, she did to me what she called "cupping" which is just a beauty-parlor term for good old orthodox spanking. After she'd gotten me in shape for the oven she took me into a shower-room and finished me up with that same hose treatment by which they subdue the recalcitrant inmates of penitentiaries.

I was then permitted to return to my sentry-box and my clothes. Once I'd recaptured my breath I felt extraordinarily full of radiant health and rugged appetite. It was time for lunch and visions of beef-steak danced in my head. But Mme. Alberta was lying in wait for me outside. "Here is your diet," she said, handing me an ominous little slip of paper which I fully expected to be marked ℞.

"I don't really care about a diet," I stammered. "You see, it isn't my weight, it's just my . . ."

"We'd like you to try it," she said.

It was a tasty little menu with the usual well done dab of chop-meat, a few fruit juices and some lettuce garnished by a rousing dressing made with mineral oil. I was to dine at the Colony that evening and could just imagine Eugene's expression if I were to ask him to bring me an order of green salad mixed with Nujol. However, I pocketed the darn thing and used the back of it for a shopping list.

Part of the system at Mme. Alberta's consists in doing quite a lot of extra curricula work. Employing the honor system, Miss Jones expects one to go through a daily routine of prescribed gymnastics at home. For this end (that end I've been referring to) she has tried to lure me into purchasing a mat of purple satin but with Jeffersonian simplicity I maintain that I can gyrate just as unsuccessfully on the moth-honored surface of my old college blanket. Exercise in the privacy of one's domicile is a brisk and splendid idea provided one has any amount of domicile and any modicum of privacy. Space in my apartment is by no means magnificent and the only reasonable expanse of it is in the living-room which in lieu of a door has an open archway and is exposed in every portion to the hall. Having no yellow Annette Kellerman at home I generally gird myself for my exertions in nothing more confining than a pair of old pink rayon bloomers. This means that whenever the door-bell rings I am obliged to leap for sanctuary behind the sofa and I don't always hear the bell—which makes it pretty fascinating for whoever comes to the door. Once, in all innocence and semi-nudity, I gave a private performance for the window-cleaner; since when, on the occasions of his monthly visit, if we have the misfortune to meet, we pass each other with lowered eyes.

A problem that confronts me more, perhaps, than most people is that much of my time is spent in travel. The rooms in the newer of what are known as the "leading" hotels are often of dimensions akin to those of a Pullman roomette. To find a sufficient number of square feet in which to spread out one's blanket and one's self becomes a problem in engineering. Often as not I have to lie with head and shoulders under the bed, one arm beneath the bureau and the other half-way across the sill of the bathroom—a pretty picture indeed for the chambermaid or house detective, should they take the notion to enter with their pass-keys. The over-shadowing proximity of furniture is a constant menace. During the course of leg-flinging, rolling upside-down, bicycling, and the rest of Miss Jones' required antics, I have cracked shins on the corners of tables, dislocated digits on the rockers of chairs, stunned myself into momentary insensibility against radiators and kicked cuspidors about like medicine balls. An important feature in reducing the—well, you know —is the thump—double thump, single thump and just plain boops-a-daisy. When executed with sufficient enthusiasm, thumping can produce considerable strain on the structure of the room and there is always the fear that the plaster in the ceiling underneath will start falling and prove fatal to some distinguished traveler like Mrs. Roosevelt or Nelson Eddy.

Reducing, if one goes by the doctrines of the Mme. Alberta school, is a twenty-four-hour job. Aside from the list of more or less stereotyped exercises, one is shown any number of everyday contortions that can, supposedly, be indulged in anywhere, any time. You can, for example, improve your posture by straightening out your spine along the edge of the nearest available door even if, to the casual observer, you appear to be scratching an itching back. You can also, while standing, do those thumps against the handiest walls—say those of the elevator, thereby bringing a moment of diversion into the monotonous life of the operator. Then there are a few less inconspicuous numbers such as standing on tiptoe and stretching up the hands ("Reaching for cherries" is Miss Jones' pretty term for it.), leaning over side-ways from the waist, deep-knee bending and a movement dignified by the name of "abdominal control" that curiously resembles the beginnings of the "danse du ventre." These you are expected to burst forth with at odd hours of the day and night even at the risk of starting the grim rumor that you're coming down with St. Vitus. Then one must walk. "Walk like a goddess" is Miss Jones' advice. So I do. I walk like mad if not particularly like a goddess. Walking in New York is a simple pursuit but in strange towns it leads to any number of surprises. Setting out for the residential section, I suddenly find myself in the thick of the colored population; or, aiming for a public park, discover that, with the uneering instinct of the homing pigeon, I'm back at the railroad yards. At other times I realize I'm striding enthusiastically down one of those streets of a nature that isn't even questionable. There remains nothing to do but hasten back to the hotel and walk round and round the block until the local policeman begins to grow suspicious.

However, all things come to her who weighs and I discover that I'm tipping the scales to a much lesser degree. Thanks to Miss Jones and Miss Svenson and my own shining determination, the last time Mme. Alberta encircled me with that glacial little measuring tape she found signs of considerable shrinkage and told me she was pleased with me— which made me glow with pride. I doubt if anyone viewing me from the neck down would as yet mistake me for Hedy Lamarr but I'm no longer so horrified by the reflection of myself in a triple mirror and what is more satisfying my clothes are beginning to look like the hand-me-downs of an older and fatter sister. And that is dejà quelque chose.

GOD REST
YOU MERRY

GOD REST YOU MERRY

MRS. JONES was awakened at an untoward hour and with a sensation of oppression and pain. The hour was seven-fifteen, the oppression was caused by Adrian, her six-year-old son, who was sitting for the most part on her chest and the pain arose from the rhythmic pounding of Adrian's fist on the side of her head.

"Time to get up, Mummy," Adrian was calling in a tone that implied she must be very far away. It would have been nice to have been far away. Mrs. Jones had stepped out the previous night with Mr. Jones and some friends from Chicago (or were they friends?) and she found it difficult to share her child's early morning exuberance. In fact, had she been an introspective person she might have been horrified to recognize in herself a sudden tendency toward infanticide . . . an abnormality apparently shared by Mr. Jones who, from the other side of the bed, raised a somewhat ghastly head, muttered, "Why don't you kill that boy?" and sank back into the state of someone just emerging from a brain operation. Mrs. Jones, collecting what she could find of herself, asked Adrian what his idea was in waking her.

"You're coming to the play!" Adrian apparently thought his mother had suddenly gone deaf.

"What play?" It seemed an odd hour for the theatre.

"The Christmas play at school, of course."

Then it all came back to her. Adrian had appeared some days ago with a mimeographed hand-bill that looked as if his entire class had walked on it, and that bore the announcement of a Christmas play to be presented by the primary class and the fond hope that at least one parent would attend . . . a veiled command to all mothers. At the time Mrs. Jones had thought it would be very nice. Even last night before going out, as she was tucking Adrian into bed, she thought it would be very sweet. Now she knew it was going to be terrible.

"What time is the play?" she croaked weakly.

"Eight-thirty. But I've got to be there at eight to get my halo on. I'm an angel." At which Mr. Jones mumbled, "Oh, yeah?" and Mrs. Jones struggled out of bed. She hadn't been in it long. In fact their home-coming taxi had pulled up at the apartment door alongside of Borden's wagon. That, she told herself, was why she felt so awful. It had nothing to do with any final night-cap at the Stork Club.

Mrs. Jones, of course, was a perfect lady. She dispatched Adrian to his room, put a couple of Alka-Seltzers in a glass to dissolve, and set about the laborious business of dressing. Mr. Jones remained comatose except for an occasional grunt and a moment when he reared up on one elbow, glared at the bubbling Alka-Seltzer and complained that "it made too damn much noise." Mrs. Jones managed to stagger first into her clothes, then into the dining-room, where she found that while she had no appetite, she had an over-whelming capacity for drinking ice-water. Adrian dismayed her by talking incessantly and scattering puffed rice about and she was further unnerved to behold through the glass of the pantry door, the baleful eye of the cook who was a fanatical teetotaler. She choked down some black coffee, sent Adrian back to his room three times to collect forgotten articles of clothing and gathered her own hat and coat. She had even the saintlike forbearance to gaze upon the recumbent form of Mr. Jones and refrain from yelling, "Sissy!" in his somewhat inflamed ear. In a daze she descended in the elevator and in a daze and a taxi rode with Adrian to school.

She felt a little shy on entering the building. Mrs. Jones was a good mother but she wasn't fanatic about it. By that I mean she didn't put in much time at Parent-Teacher's meetings, nor was she one to pay frequent calls on the head master for the sake of discussing Adrian's sense of Group-Consciousness. In fact, except for the opening day, she hadn't set foot in the place. She was determined, however, to make a gracious impression. An elderly gentleman standing just inside the door exchanged greetings with Adrian. Mrs. Jones, thinking he looked distinguished, extended her hand and in a voice that she forced to be bright said: "How do you do? I'm Adrian's mother."

The gentleman hesitated then silently took her hand while Adrian collapsed with mortification against a statue of Zeus.

"Mother!" he hissed (he never called her Mother unless he was particularly ashamed of her), "that's Bill, the janitor!" Mrs. Jones repressed the impulse to say, "Then what the hell's he doing here?" and with what dignity she could muster followed the rapidly retreating figure of her son.

"Where do I go, Adrian?" she panted, feeling as she did her first day of freshman year. Adrian waved his school-bag in a wild gesture that might have meant anything and vanished through a door. At the end of the corridor a number of women were being ushered into a room by a young master who looked awfully pure and unjaded. Still smarting from the janitor episode she was hesitant to inform him about being Adrian's mother. Judging by the way she must look it would be giving Adrian a break to keep her identity secret. So she merely smiled and the young man smiled back and told her to go in and just take any seat. A classroom had been converted into a theatre with rows of chairs facing an improvised stage. Mrs. Jones selected a position toward the back and near a door. It being an affair of the Primary class, the chairs were those designed for little tots, Mrs. Jones was a tall gal and when she sat down her knees came up somewhere in the vicinity of her chin.

She looked at her watch and sighed. Twenty minutes to wait. Perhaps she should have gone with Adrian to help him with his halo. But who was she to deal with haloes this bleak morning? She must try to get herself into the spirit of Yuletide and little children, however hard. Snatches of music she'd heard at the Stork Club kept running through her head, and her head was in no condition to have anything run through it except a few cool mountain streams. She had a very awful pain at the back of her neck and her eyes felt like freshly dipped Easter eggs. Moreover, her heart was thumping in an alarming way. She told herself this was stage-fright for Adrian.

In misery she gazed at the stage. The curtain, which sagged badly in the middle, gave indications of violent activity on the Thespian side. It fluttered and bulged and kept coming apart until an adult hand reached out and secured it with a safety pin. The room began to fill with mothers, governesses and a few protesting fathers. A young woman in a tweed suit plopped herself down in the adjacent seat. She looked annoyingly clear-eyed and healthy . . . obviously one of those splendid mothers who take courses in vital subjects and go in for exercise as if it were a Cause. She smiled energetically at Mrs. Jones and said, "Your boy in this?" in the cheery voice of a Girl Scout Captain.

Mrs. Jones nodded wanly and at the same time edged slightly away. It hadn't been so long since she'd had that last night-cap and (degrading thought!) she hadn't thought to chew any coffee-beans.

"Both my sons are taking part." The woman talked like a Roman matron. "I have twins."

She would have, Mrs. Jones reflected and thought how fearful it would have been to have been aroused by two Adrians this morning. She managed to cheep, "How lovely," and the woman asked what was her little boy's name. On being informed she said, "Oh" in a tone that hinted darkly that she knew him all right. "He's Primary One B, isn't he?" she continued. Mrs. Jones considered it pretty nosey of this woman to know more about Adrian than she herself did but she said she guessed he was and were her twins in the same division? "Oh, dear, no, they're a whole class ahead." Then as an afterthought, "They're a year younger than Adrian." Mrs. Jones started to bridle but it hurt to bridle so she sank back into her state of moral apathy, reflecting moodily that considering his heritage it was only just retribution that her child should be a mental defective. A new arrival took the chair on the other side. Influenced by the community spirit of the mother of the twins, Mrs. Jones essayed a feeble grin and said "How do you do?" The woman returned a stiff salutation in the unmistakable accents of an English governess . . . the superior variety to whom misguided Americans pay a hundred a month to turn their domestic household into living hell. The situation was eased by the entrance of the piano teacher followed by a line of little boys bearing cymbals, tambourines, triangles and other instruments of

torture. The entrance of the orchestra coincided with that of a group that looked to be a bevy of green and red elves but turned out to be a portion of the Primary glee club clad as choristers.

The footlights went on and the rest of the room was in darkness. A murmur of fatuous anticipation arose from the rows of beaming mothers but nothing else happened. The piano teacher rose and in a loud hiss told some unknown behind the scenes that they'd put out his light, too, whereat all the lights went on again and the mothers laughed good-naturedly. After considerable snapping of buttons and some playful going on and off of side brackets, the desired effect was obtained and an impressive chord struck on the piano.

The opening selection was "God rest you, merry gentlemen" sung in sweet treble by the glee club and punctuated by the orchestra who, on words like *"dismay* and "Christmas *Day"* came forth with a goodly wallop of tympany. The mother of the twins looked happy and said wasn't it darling and Mrs. Jones concurred, although in her private opinion, it was more like gems from "Hellzapoppin." After the carol there was a pause and then the curtains were yanked as far as they'd go with the safety pin still holding them. They were then yanked back and the fastening removed, all of which convulsed the choristers. Finally the curtains opened on a bare stage and a pause that turned into an awkward stage wait. There were sounds of scrambling and a juvenile voice distinctly said, "Cut it out, will ya?" At length there entered from the left three rather diminutive Magi, orientally splendid in glazed muslin, bearing their respective gifts on sofa-cushions. The scene was in pantomime, the glee-club furnishing the narrative with a rendering of "We Three Kings of Orien-*Tar*." There seemed to be some difference of opinion in regard to the locality of the star. One looked before him, one searched the audience like a veteran actor counting the house, and one looked directly overhead until his crown started to slip off, whereat he lowered his gaze to the ground. The Roman matron nudged her and pointed out one of her Gracchi. He was, of course, the only one acting correctly. The scene closed with the finish of the carol. At the curtain one or two of the spectators ventured gentle applause but were shushed by the rest who regarded it somewhat in the nature of a performance of "Parsifal." During the entr'acte the English governess leaned over and asked if she'd had her boy bring his own costume. She replied why no that she understood the school furnished them. The governess made a face like Beatrice Lillie making a face like a governess, and said yes, but *she* never let *her* charge wear something that had gone the rounds goodness *how* long, and Mrs. Jones wondered morbidly if she'd better start watching Adrian for symptoms of Bubonic Plague.

The second scene was reminiscent of the first, it being in this instance a case of shepherds instead of kings and the theme song being "While Shepherds watched their Flocks." On a table disguised as a celestial promontory there appeared a small angel who made beckoning gestures and the finale was considerably enlivened by the angel's little sister who from the audience emitted a joyful, "Why there's Brud!" The second intermission was very long. From backstage came sounds of shuffling feet and of heavy things being dragged forth . . . possibly bodies. The curtains would seem about to part, then would ease up, amid muffled cries of, "No, wait!" The choristers threw in a carol or two as a filler. Adrian's big moment was approaching and Mrs. Jones' hands became clammy. Finally all was ready and there was presented a really very charming Nativity tableau. The Manger with its participants was at one side while in the background on and around the same table as that of act two, a close-ranked host of angels gave an impression that Heaven was at the moment slightly overcrowded.

"That's my other twin playing Joseph," her neighbor whispered. Mrs. Jones nodded and noted with satisfaction that one side of his beard was noticeably unstuck. For a time she looked vainly for Adrian. After

a bit in the back row she spotted a cherub whose dia-
bolical behavior made her recognize her son. Half
hidden from view he had a vantage place over his
sanctified buddies whom, judging by their wriggling
and squirming, he was pinching in their all too mortal
rears. She could only hope the All-American mother
hadn't noticed but she had, for she said, "Why there's
Adrian." Then added, "Restless type, isn't he?" Adrian's pastimes were cut short by some unseen authority
in the wings and for one carol he remained comparatively tranquil. He looked very sweet, Mrs. Jones
thought, except for the fact that his halo was cocked
at the angle of a gob's hat. It was apparently loose and
he eventually discovered that he could do all sorts of
fascinating things with it. As it was about to slide off
one ear, a violent jerk would bring it back, while a few
vigorous nods would throw it into a sort of spin. To
Mrs. Jones it seemed as if all eyes were fixed on her
appalling child. Beside him the Principals in the
drama paled into insignificance. She prayed fervently
for some cataclysm that would wipe out both herself
and Adrian at once. It looked as if her prayers were
about to be granted, at least in part, for after a few
minutes of fiendish head-waggling the angel quite
suddenly and unexpectedly fell from view in the tradition of Lucifer.

-€ 84 ∋-

Mrs. Jones waited to hear those all too familiar bellows but there followed so complete a silence she began to think that perhaps it was a case of concussion. However, in a second, that same adult arm was stretched forth and she could make out the huddled-up form of her son being dragged ignominiously from the boards. This was her cue to make an exit also. The play was nearing its finish and she thought it best to make a quick get-away. As she stumbled out, the choir was again singing "God Rest You Merry Gentlemen," the audience being asked to join in. She heard herself singing her own version which began, "God help you, weary gentlemen."

In the corridor she was met by Adrian. Far from looking contrite he was all smiles—

"Hi, Mum," he called serenely, "how did you like it?" The words of vituperation died on her lips. She said she liked it very much. Adrian beamed.

"Did you see me?" he asked.

"Yes, dear," she said. "Where do we go to get a cab?"

PARODIES

FOR WHOM THE GONG SOUNDS

(With apologies, somewhat, to Mr. Hemingway)

ROBERT JORDAN snapped the lock of his revolver, made certain the machine-gun at his hip was handy, gripped his màquina and continued to crawl up the Guadarrama hills on his belly. Robert Jordan grinned. You're almost there, he told himself. He'd been telling himself things like that all day. Robert Jordan was hunching over a rocky ledge now, hanging on by the bristles of his chest. The warm Spanish earth scraped his belly. Robert Jordan could feel a pine-cone in his navel. It was a resinous pine-cone, the kind they grow in Catalan. These people,

Robert Jordan thought, turn out to be people. There's no getting away from that. Sure there isn't. Hell, no.

A gypsy was sitting on a rock strumming a guitar. With one bare foot he practiced range-finding with a sub-machine gun. The other foot lay idly on his màquina. The gypsy's face was the color of old Virginia ham.

"Salud," Robert Jordan said.

Fernando eyed him through the barrel of a Lewis gun. Robert Jordan made certain his Mauser was uncocked. The gypsy's voice was like golden Amontillado gurgling out of a wineskin.

"Thou wast of the street car, camarada?"

"Comé no? Why not?" Robert Jordan thought of the last street car he had blown up. They had found arms and legs all over the roofs. One femur had gone as far as Valladolid.

"Quien sabe," said Jacinto. "Who knows."

"Each according to each," said Ignacio. "Street cars I have a boredom of. We have heard what we have heard. Si. Yes." He flung some hand grenades into a nose-bag, trampling them firmly with his rope-soled feet.

"Hombre," said Anselmo, squinting down the barrel of a 45mm. gun. "One goes to the cave."

"Bueno," said Robert Jordan. "Good."

Robert Jordan and the gypsy continued to scrabble up the hill past a deserted saw-mill. Juanito burrowed his way, Andalusian fashion, into a pile of saw-dust, and emerged after a little while, grinning sweatily. Robert Jordan opened his pack, making sure that all was as it had been. He unlocked the grommet, untied the drawstrings, uncoiled the insulating wire and tossed the caber. His groping fingers came in reassuring contact with a bunch of bayonets. His automatic pistols were safe, so were the hand grenades, the old French '75 and his father's sawed-off shot-gun. His father had been a preacher, a man of God back in Ohio. He drew forth a bottle of TNT and a quart of Haig and Haig. It might come in handy when the time came for blowing up the boardwalk. He studied the bottle of Haig and Haig and thought, no. They'll take me for a fascist. A bloody fascist, that's what they'll take me for. He put the bottle of Haig and Haig back into the bandolier of ammunition, screwing it down with a grenade pin, a belaying pin and a Skull and Bones pin. Then he got out a magnum of Courvoisier. This is more their stuff, he said to himself. Then to make sure, he pulled out a carton of Abdullas and a box of Corona Coronas. That was all he had in his knapsack except, of course, his sleeping bag, a case of Old Grandad, three pairs of rope-soled shoes and an asbestos suit for when he blew up the boardwalk.

An old man sat at the mouth of the cave guarding the entrance with a Mauser, a Howitzer, a Winchester and a Fly-swatter.

"Salud, camarada," said the old man.

"Equally," said Robert Jordan, then added, "Hola!" for good measure.

"Thou. Thou wast of the street-car?"

"Wast."

He is old, Robert Jordan said to himself. And the gypsy is old, too, and some day I will be old. But I'm not old yet, not yet, I'm not old.

"He knows of which whereof he speaks of, old one," the gypsy was saying.

"Que va, young one."

"It makes well to joke, old one."

"Pass, middle-aged one."

————————

The mouth of the cave was camouflaged by a curtain of saddle-blankets, matadores' capes and the soles of old espadrilles. Inside it smelt of man-sweat, acrid and brown . . . horse-sweat sweet and magenta. There was the leathery smell of leather and the coppery smell of copper and borne in on the clear night air came the distant smell of skunk.

The wife of Pablo was stirring frijoles in a Catalonian wineskin. She wore rope-soled shoes and a belt of hand grenades. Over her magnificent buttocks swung a 16th Century cannon taken from the Escorial.

"I obscenity in the obscenity of thy unprintable obscenity," said Pilar.

"This is the Ingles of the street car. He of the board-walk to come soon."

"I obscenity in the unprintable of the milk of all street cars." The woman was stirring the steaming mess with the horns of a Mura bull. She stared at Robert Jordan then smiled. "Obscenity, obscenity, obscenity," she said, not unkindly.

"Que va," said Robert Jordan. "Bueno. Good."

"Menos mal," said El Sordo. "Not so good."

"Go unprint thyself," said Pilar. The gypsy went outside and unprinted himself.

The girl with the shaved head filled a tin pail full of petite marmite and handed it to him and she gave him a great swig from the wine-skin and he chewed the succulent bits of horsemeat and they said nothing.

And now Esteban stood beside him on the rim of

the gorge. This is it, Robert Jordan said to himself. I believe this is it. I did not think it was this to be it but it seems to be it, alright. Robert Jordan spat down the gorge. Pablo watched the fast disappearing globule of man-saliva then slowly, softly spat down the gorge. Pilar said obscenity thy saliva then she too spat down the gorge. This time it was Pablo's gorge.

———

The girl was walking beside him.

"Hola, Ingles," she said. "Hello, English."

"Equally, guapa," said Robert Jordan.

"Que va," said the girl.

"Rabbit."

Robert Jordan pulled the pistol lanyard up, cocked his màquina and tightened the ropes of his rope-soled shoes.

"Vamos," he said. "Let's go."

"Si," said Maria. "Yes."

They walked on in silence until they came to a rocky ledge. There were rough rocks and thistles and a wild growth of Spanish dagger. Robert Jordan spread his buffalo robe out for himself and allowed Maria to lie near him on a bed of nettles. The earth moved.

"Rabbit," said Robert Jordan. "Hast aught?"

"Nay, naught."

"Maria," he said. "Mary. Little shaved head."

"Let me go with thee and be thy rabbit."

The earth moved again. This time it was a regular earthquake. Californians would have called it a temlor.

Robert Jordan had reached the boardwalk. He lay in the gorse and rubble. He had his infernal machine beside him, some hand grenades, a blunderbuss, an arquebus and a greyhound bus. His màquina was held securely in his teeth. Across the ravine Anselmo was sniping off sentries as they passed.

Listen, Robert Jordan said to himself, only the fascist bombs made so much noise he couldn't hear. You had to do what you did. If you don't do what you do now you'll never do what you do now. Not now you won't. Goltz was right. A real surprise surprised people. Sure it does. He lashed the wire through the rings of the cotter pins of the release levers of the wires of the main spring of the coil, insulating it with a piece cut off the bottom of his rope-soled shoes.

What about the others . . . Eladio and Ignacio . . . Anselmo and St. Elmo? And Rabbit? I wonder how Rabbit is. Stop that now. This is no time to think about Rabbit . . . Or rabbits. Better think about something else. Think about llamas. It's better to breathe, he thought. It's always much better to breathe. Sure it is. The time was gradually, inevitably drawing near. Someone in the valley was singing an old Catalonian song. A plane crashed quietly overhead. Robert Jordan lay still and listened for the gong to sound.

A SMATTERING OF ARROGANCE

A SMATTERING OF ARROGANCE

*Being Excerpts from the recent Best-Seller
of Bosco Durant*

. . . The winter I lived in New York I was constantly meeting a number of the younger composers . . . Schtengel, Schtingel, Schmalz and that strange product of Armenia, City College and the Hearst Ranch, Anton Tifflis, who used kitchenware, carpet-sweepers and acousticon-batteries for his effects. Tifflis used to say he could outfit an entire symphony orchestra in Bloomingdale's basement. He had just conducted his occupational jazz-sonata *Strepticoccus* before the MacDowell Club. That was the season the famous quarrel between Katz and Blatz occurred. Katz said Blatz's music was

Ethelbert Nevin on saxophones and Blatz over-heard him. The language that ensued would make Steinbeck read like Laura Jean Libby. This took place in the Long Island house of a rich society dame who liked to feed hungry composers, so of course no-body paid any attention to the hostess. Just as Blatz was about to crown Katz with a viola d'amore, Harpo Marx saved the situation by striking up *The Rosary* on the harp and a talent scout who happened to be there signed up the act for Paramount.

I remember Mrs. Vanderbilt was among the also-rans. Earlier in the evening she'd approached me with the question, "Mr. Durant, what's it like to be a com-poser?"

"Mrs. Vanderbilt," I countered, "what's it like to be a Vanderbilt?" But she didn't get it.

I've known all the conductors there are to know and some there aren't. Siegfried Himmelblitzen of Ber-lin, Henri Fraise-des-Bois of Paris, Tutti fan Frutti of Milan, and Colin Colin of London. There was the fiery Russian conductor Lvwoff who terrified his men, and gentle little Jan Janje of Holland who was so afraid of the musicians' union he'd stop on his way to rehearsal to be psycho-analyzed before he dared face his orchestra. The well-known incident of Toscanini

and the oboe-player is one that has gone down in musical history. During a rehearsal of the young Magyar
composer Czskmvo's tone-poem *Arnica 3* in the midst
of the intricate dynamics of the sustained tutti Bob-
kin, the oboist played a c flat instead of a b natural.
The maestro stopped the orchestra, fixed the wretched
man with a withering stare and called out, "Bodkin!
You steenk!" On another occasion at a performance
of the League of Composers, Dr. Stowkowski, ever
with an eye for effects, made a startling entrance
through the large end of a bass-horn.

I remember a party at Benny de Buddy's. Everyone was there . . . Jimmy Dorsey, Schoenberg, Eddy
Duchin, Sam Goldwyn, Sir Thomas Beecham and
Edna Ferber. There was a lot to drink and some of
the gang had brought along some extra pianos. There
were four in all. We placed them so that the keyboards
formed a square and I sat in the middle playing all
four at once. Later I was joined by Deems Taylor,
Bobby Dolan and Georges Enesco. We all sat on the
same stool and improvised a toccata we called *Rump
Steak*. Around four A.M. some of the neighbors
started to complain. We called out, "O.K., we'll give
you a lullaby," and went into an eight-handed capric-
cioso, Deems playing a bit of *Midsummer Night's*

Dream, Bobby *Broadway Lullaby,* Enesco *Just a Baby's Prayer at Twilight,* while I wove the themes together with *I've Got Rhythm* in melodic overtones, cacophonic undertones and a lush contrapuntal crescendo. I later re-orchestrated this for a film called "Little Miss Girlie," a "B" picture that deserved better rating. To return to the four-piano party. Some stuffed shirt living at the River House eventually sent round the police, so we merely moved the drinks and the pianos down onto an empty coal barge that had been moored to the Yacht Club landing since the depression, and continued to serenade the rich son-of-a-gun with *Brother, Can You Spare a Dime?*

———————

I had composed a sinfonietta and was rather anxious to have the opinion of my good friend and fellow-genius, Herman Glitz. I tracked him down one evening at the Algonquin and played it for him. For some time he said nothing. I was in an agony of suspense.

"Well?" I asked nervously.

"Let's go to Elsa Maxwell's party," was his only reply. We went. There were a lot of theatrical people there. During the evening Charlie Mac Arthur came up to me and with a faun-like leer that would have gone well in the "Sacre du Printemps" said, "Durant,

Glitz says your new piece is a cross between Palestrina and the Sweet Singer of Michigan." I left abruptly just as they were all starting to play a game in which everybody had to impersonate a famous article of furniture. It was a month before I got my revenge. When Glitz was conducting the first performance of his *Aphrodite at Coney Island* I had a large bowl of guppies passed up to him on the podium.

I had made a niche for myself in the musical world and was now ready for something big. Finally it came. I landed the enviable job of "end-title" writer for Hal Roach. I'd never been to Hollywood and didn't know where to stay. Moreover, to rent a house or even to live in a hotel costs money. I wired Buzzy X . . . the former Follies beauty and Hollywood's most sought-after hostess . . . if she'd like to have me come visit her. She wired back "No, I wouldn't." So I rushed to Los Angeles on the "Chief" and out to Buzzy's villa at Santa Monica in a taxi (I made her butler pay the fare) and moved right into a billiard room on the ground floor, which I turned into a studio. Buzzy came home that evening and finding me drinking her Napoleon brandy said, "Bosco Durant! What are you doing here?"

"Drinking brandy," I replied calmly. That was

January 5th. I stayed until the following Christmas when my contract expired. Buzzy kept putting me out and I kept coming back. Buzzy tried to run a sort of salon for the so-called intelligentsia but I managed to put a spoke in that. When people came into the house I, from my ground floor studio, would entice them in to see me instead, luring them with the sort of music I knew each could not resist . . . for Schoenberg, *Chop-Sticks;* for Salvadore Dali, Stephen Foster; for Alexander Woollcott and for the rest, pure Durant. Poor Buzzy up in her Frank Lloyd Wright drawing room. She'd wait all day on a zebra skin and nobody gave her a thought!

―――――――

Those were stimulating evenings. Everybody came and everybody talked in clichés. . . . H. G. Wells, Jack Dempsey, Fannie Brice, Margalo Gillmore, Ben Hecht . . . they all came flocking. The Marx Brothers would occasionally drop in, usually from the roof. People are always talking about the Marx Brothers but to my way of thinking the best comment about them was made by George Kauffman. "They make me laugh," he said.

The brilliant young composer, Butch Ginsberg, would sometimes saunter in. After a successful season at Bayreuth and the Scala he had come to Hollywood to write "insert" music for Shirley Temple. "Things," he used to say, "are being done out here."

One evening Jesse Lasky came to see Buzzy and, as always happened, ended by spending the evening with me. Marlene Dietrich was present. Her film, "The Letch of Algiers," had just been released and in the course of the evening she said to Lasky, "You liked my picture, no?" Lasky said "NO" and walked out. We all laughed.

After six months Buzzy and I finally made up our differences and when Lord and Lady Mountbatten came to the Coast, Buzzy gave them a party to which I invited all my friends. Buzzy received us in a poncho. When the Mountbattens were announced she took it off and went to meet them in Garbo's old Mata Hari costume. It was her way of introducing them to good solid American humor.

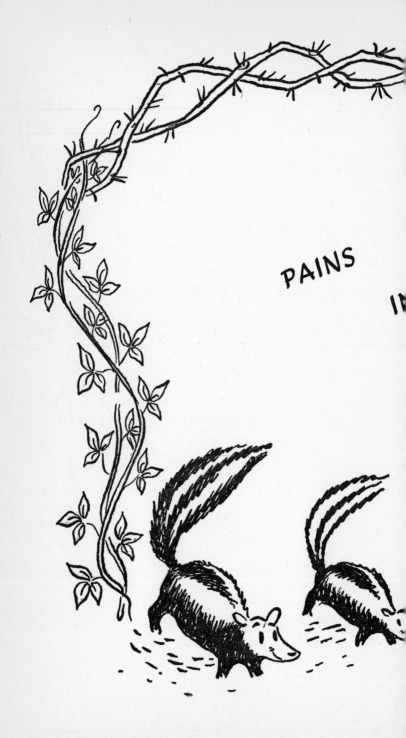

PAINS

I

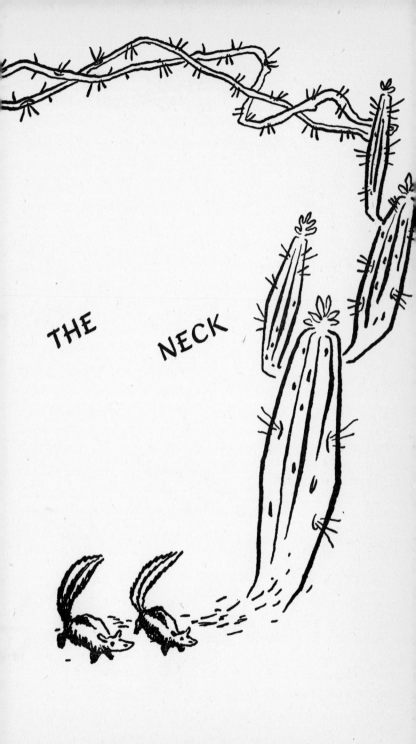

THE NECK

THIS UP-LIFT STUFF

NOTHING can depress me more rapidly nor more hopelessly than a book on how to be happy. I am by nature an optimist and until the popular tracts on how to get that way began to flood the market, it never occurred to me whether I was that way or not. The spectacular success of these little volumes is sufficient proof that the world at large is in dire need of such messages of hope and my normally cheerful nature is gradually being soured by the suspicion that I, too, am unhappy but have never been bright enough to realize it. It's the same story as someone asking you, when you're feeling exceptionally well, if you haven't been over-working. I don't go in for such literature voluntarily. To purchase it would shame me very badly and ever to be caught reading it gives me that old sense of guilt with which I whisked the latest copy of *Snappy Stories* under my pillow when the dormitory proctor was making her rounds. However, every now and then one of these messages of joy, health and business-promotion turns up in somebody's guest-room and goaded by the morbid curiosity to learn why for six months it has headed the best-seller list, I open it when I think nobody's looking. It is usually an at-tractively gotten up affair with a gay jacket and sometimes marginal drawings of a whimsical nature. The author's style is either that of the bright young thing with a flair for epigram or the optimistic hearty who writes as if on brisk mornings he also announced radio setting-up exercises. In either case the general tone is that things aren't as bad as you think they are, and if you're like me and have never thought they were, you immediately begin to think that perhaps they are.

The opening chapter is either a cheerful survey of the mental state of four-fifths of society with some reassuring title like "Why Commit Suicide?" or "Hi there, Manic Depressive!" or else it's a little excursion into autobiography wherein the author comes clean about his (or more usually *her*) past existence of failure, heebie-jeebies and general social leprosy. It starts off in such an atmosphere of sick-of-it-allness, I, for one, find myself contracting the contagion and

wondering moodily if they ever took women in the Foreign Legion . . . (And I don't mean what you mean, either!) Having begun by shattering the reader's spirit, the author sets about repairing it with as much success as Junior, who has just taken his father's watch to pieces. Their method is to proclaim a *Solution* . . . simple, but great, which came to them as a sort of up-to-date but miraculous Revelation. After which life began anew . . . which in some instances seems too bad. The Great Solution is generally a sort of catch-phrase which any good advertising man might have thought up, but which the publishers in their blurbs hail as the greatest discovery since polaroid. The phrase is something such as "I am not sad, I am very, very happy" or "Fear is nuts" or "If at first you don't succeed, try something else." The idea being that you repeat this to yourself in all crises such as when you're called up before the boss, or when your husbands steps out with a blonde, or when you find yourself face to face with an escaped tiger. It is an addakadabra by means of which you may overnight become a combination of Greta Garbo, Doris Duke and Frances Perkins . . . (That is, if you care to.) The first chapter having completely blasted my morale, this therapy seems the only hope and I start muttering the magic phrase with the frenzy of despair. For all the difference it makes I might as well be repeating, "Remember the Maine." It only makes things worse.

If the "you-too-can-achieve-happiness" sort of literature crushes my animal spirits what those psychiatry books do to me is nobody's business . . . except, perhaps, the psychiatrists'. They, I am convinced, turn out this stuff for the purpose of increasing their clientèle. For years I've gone my simple way, assuming myself to be more or less normal . . . a frail whimsey which the perusal of any book on psychoanalysis will knock into a cocked hat. I might as well give up and let them start measuring me for a strait-jacket. Prior to the fad for works on "Popular Psychology" (Odd nomenclature! why not "Popular Cholera?") I never gave my mind any more thought than I gave my heart, my lungs or my state senator. It was just something that was there. But now it appears mine isn't there at all. Or if it is, it's in a critical condition. The irony of it all is that after page after page of scientific and psychological miasma the gist of everything seems to be (and any old farmer's wife might have told you, calling it "horse-sense") that you can't control your thoughts anyway and the best thing to do is pay no attention to them. But by that time I am paying desperate and jibbering attention. My everyday characteristics seem to be listed under headings indicative of melancholia, kleptomania and paranoia. As for those horrifying case histories collected like bibliography at the end, they are all too indicative of how I shall doubtlessly end up. The woman who was rushed off to a sana-tarium because she became obsessed by a certain tune is me all over with *The Music Goes Round and Round,* which it did for weeks and will even now if given the least encouragement. I was ever and still am a good sleeper, with the unpleasant exception of an interlude of insomnia that came as a result of reading the case history of the fellow whose slumber was untroubled until he got worrying about it and who hasn't slept more than one hour a night since. This wakefulness might have continued indefinitely had I not shortly afterward been enlivened by the story of another psychopath whose little dementia was to lie in bed all day in a self-imposed doze, after which I had to be tided over a mild attack of sleeping-sickness. The young mother who consulted an analyst only to learn that she loved a cocker span-iel more than she loved her child frightened me for weeks. I have a spaniel . . . also a child . . . and in my zeal to prove to myself that I wasn't becoming like this unnatural monster, I treated the spaniel with such indifference and lavished such outbursts of violent affection on the child, the one went into a decline and the other fled from me in terror.

The best course, naturally, is to avoid all such read-ing. But it's like avoiding looking at a street accident.

However, I too have discovered my own Great Solution. If up-lift books cast me down, those of pessimism and despair work the other way. I've just finished Dostoyevsky's "Idiot" and haven't felt so bucked up in weeks. There you are! An idea for the next best seller. Incidentally, I claim 75% of the gross.

YOUTH'S
FURNISHINGS

YOUTH'S FURNISHINGS

THE day arrives in the life of every son's mother when, looking across the breakfast table at her offspring, she realizes that not only has he reached the stage when he needs new clothes, he has stretched out well beyond it. His coat looks as if it were intended for a bell-hop and the sleeves have become so short anyone might think he'd pushed them back for the purpose of washing his hands . . . anyone, that is, who doesn't know small boys. His shirt-tails can no longer be confined below his vest, his collar, if buttoned, would strangle him and his shorts live up to their name in a manner almost

indecent. His ties have started growing whiskers
and although she is at the moment spared the horrid
sight, she knows that underneath this inadequate
outer covering his underwear has shrunk to the rip-
ping point and his socks are out at every toe, like
mitts. Even his shoes are the sort one finds along
beaches. With a little boy everything goes to pieces
at once and he emerges from all his clothing with
the inevitability, if not the beauty, of the moth from
the chrysalis. To complicate things, this metamor-
phosis always takes place at an unseasonable time
of year when it is too cool for summer garments to
do anything but give him pneumonia and when winter clothes seem to induce symptoms of scarlet fever
in the tiny wearer. The only sensible solution would
be to put the child to bed for the interim. However,
every mother drags her protesting son to the boy's
department of the most convenient emporium and
attempts in one fell shopping-trip to do what is
known as "outfit" him for the approaching season.
It's a bad day for all concerned and one that proves
to be a severe test of mother-love and filial piety
with both these tender emotions exhibiting alarming indications of snapping.

The mother starts in by announcing in tones of
forced gladness, trying to make it sound like an in-

vitation to a barbecue, that they're going to go shopping and won't it be fun. The little boy who knows darn well it won't be, meets the suggestion with a barrage of protest. He thinks of urgent things he has to do, he invents engagements with fictitious buddies in the park, he insists he has to get his homework done, he complains of a headache, he even goes so far as to say he feels like spending the morning practicing his scales on whatever instrument he happens to afflict his family with. The mother, steeling herself, remains adamant and sends the child off for his cap and coat. He obeys with the alacrity of a reluctant snail, all the while muttering baleful words to the effect that he hates those old stores anyway, he hates getting those old clothes, he hates all that old shopping, and pale but determined, she bundles him off before "old mothers" are added to the category of anathema.

In my household these crises arise about twice a year. I try my best to make it as painless as possible. I select a near-by department store and a time of day when the crowds will be few. I give solemn oaths that it won't take long; I even dangle the News Reel and a double-chocolate-frosted-peppermint-whatever as rewards for submissive behavior. It does little good. After muttering a violent "phooey" which is his equivalent for darkest blasphemy, he sets forth in a black mood which no subsequent occurrence is likely to dissipate. He regards all mankind as his enemy. Even the local taxi-driver, with whom he is usually on rotarian terms, is in league against him. The store, when finally we reach it, he considers an edifice planned and constructed solely for the purpose of annoying him and succeeding beyond the architect's most savage dreams. Everything is very awful to him . . . the display of merchandise on the ground floor, which in his contempt he is apt to brush off when passing counters, leaving me to pick up and face the saleswoman who clearly takes us for a light-fingered team; the elevators jammed with shoppers onto whose feet he has an unfortunate way of backing, the necessity for removing his cap and overcoat and then the inhuman cruelty of being made to carry them. Added to his exasperation is a profound shame for his mother who displays what he considers an embarrassing inability to locate the various departments. I try to divert him by switching from the lift to the escalator for which he has invented a little pastime of his own which consists in gaining the middle of the incline and sticking there, jumping rhythmically down one step at a time in the same technique as the Ben Hur chariot race and involving some pretty lively encounters with ascending passengers. Even this distraction palls. From the moment of the first shove of the revolving door he has begun saying, "When are we going to go?" and he keeps it up like a leitmotif in tones that range from those of fiery aggressiveness to heartbreaking pathos. Eventually we reach the boy's department and I assure him that with a little co-operation and fortitude on his part, it won't take long. For a moment he shows signs of becoming moderately resigned to the inevitable, then some misguided salesman approaches him with the best of intentions and a much too cheerful smile and calls him "Sonny," whereat he reverts to his mood of homeric wrath. I must admit I too am discomfited by these alert young men who behave as if they'd just received a citation from Dale Carnegie. Their high-pressure friendliness gets me down. I feel I should start things off by shaking hands with them and inquiring after their little sister. They seem to expect the average mother to act and talk as if she'd stepped off the front page of *Good Housekeeping*. And what's worse, I do. I find myself looking tenderly maternal and in a voice of treacle saying, "How do you do. I'm looking for a suit (as if I'd mislaid it somewhere). It's for my little boy." It wouldn't be much of a surprise to hear myself referring to him as "my bairn."

"And what age is the youngster?" the salesman asks in the bright manner of a Scout Master. To my child "youngster" is as much fighting language as "Sonny" and he retreats to a vantage position behind the folds of my coat, glowering like Achilles from his tent.

I am not by nature the chatty type, yet I find that for some reason I unburden myself to this repulsive young man at an alarming rate. I tell him the boy's age, adding with the happy pride of the mother of an Asbury Park prize baby that he wears two sizes larger. At which the salesman says, "Well, well, you'd never guess it, now, would you?" And I echo fatuously, "No you wouldn't, now, would you?" I explain how rapidly he's growing and how he takes after his father. I tell what grade he's in or about to be dropped from. If I had one of his English compositions with me I'd probably exhibit it. This flow of confidences continues during the selection of clothes. I describe what sort of things he'll need for the country and why, and in connection with things like corduroy pants I hear myself coming forth with such tender confessions as, "My little boy is very susceptible to poison ivy." My child listens to this just long enough to become more ashamed than ever of his mother, then disappears.

It is remarkable with what suddenness little boys in stores can vanish into thin air. They wander off to distant departments, one sees the tops of their heads setting behind far-off counters, then when one rushes over to get them, they're no longer there. They venture out through doors marked EXIT and stay so long one is about to put in a police alarm when they come strolling back from a completely opposite direction. They discover appalling things to do such as spinning revolving tie-racks or opening and shutting those deep hat-bins, into one of which they drop their gloves and promptly forget which one it was. At intervals they are retrieved and brought back to the scene of their tribulation where they express their boredom by flinging themselves across the nearest glass show-counter which, because God is good, fails to shatter under the impact.

Suits and a coat being the most important items and the only ones for which the presence of the child is essential, I try to procure them at the start and we each have decided and divergent views on what we want. I imagine all sons and mothers come to blows over the matter of choice of apparel. With her inherent instinct for "keeping him young as long as possible" the average parent is hard put to it not to select attire that the average child considers a gross insult to his years. Certainly, were I to follow my own inclinations, I'd dress my boy like Peter Pan until he were ready for Harvard. His taste, on the other hand, runs to garments not only far too old for him but absolutely mortician sobriety. Given his choice, he'd with rapture set forth to school every morning in a Prince Albert. Along with these soberly conventional tastes goes an alarming love of things like leather helmets that have goggles on them, western belts made in Japan and tasty wind-breakers adorned with the portraits of such celebrities as Dopey and Mickey Mouse. It would scarcely surprise me to see him some day appear for a children's party in his best dark-blue suit, patent pumps, a carnation in his button-hole and a white cloth cap that says "Purina Chows."

Finally we manage to compromise on something neither of us likes very much and I then drag him under protest to the fitting-room. Here we immure ourselves, the bright young salesman, the tailor, my child and myself in a diminutive cubicle which gives one the sensation of trying to fit something in an overcrowded elevator. If the keep-smiling salesman has succeeded in making me go folksey the tailor who is usually a taciturn individual with no lighter moments has an insidious way of shaming me. His professional pride is at stake, he always wants the suit to fit, whereas I hold out for its being an accurate size too large so the child can "grow into it." I try to make my tone convey the fact that though simple folk we still are proud but the man clearly considers us small-time custom. Then there is that awkward moment when, blushing prettily, I hear myself saying, "Are you sure it's big enough in the . . . has he enough room . . . er. Darling (this to the small boy), just lean over a moment, will you?"

During the fitting my son alternately groans, sighs, complains of overwhelming fatigue and repeats his "When are we going to go?" refrain. He swipes a piece of chalk from the tailor and for a last-resource pastime begins to mark up the walls. I remonstrate feebly and the salesman, still smiling, says, "There's nothing like a boy, is there?" And I answer, "No, thank God!"

Our next stop is the shoe department. Here my offspring lies in a state of collapse half on the chair, half over the stool. He can just bring himself to thrust his foot into the shoe clerk's discouraged face and with what little energy is left in him, he improves the time producing sort of castanet effects with a couple of wooden foot measurers. After shoes, we head for the underwear department although from the complaints of my appendage we ought by right to be heading for the Bellevue Emergency ward. During the course of this trek, in the manner of a hare in a paper chase, he manages to scatter behind him cap, scarf, gloves, the cap pistol he's brought along in case of attack and finally his coat which for most of the time he's been dragging after him, holding it by one of the cuffs. One by one I salvage them and turn myself into a beast of burden. By now his wrath has subsided into pitiful hopelessness. His is the resigned air of someone who knows he's not long for this world. As a matter of fact I begin to get alarmed about him myself. He appears to be growing very weak and is deathly pallid except for a hectic flush on either cheekbone. I place an anxious hand on his neck and it seems to me definitely feverish. I start imagining he's "coming down" with something in its most virulent form. The shopping list still shows any number of items not as yet crossed off . . . but in a panic I let them go. We board the first elevator with a DOWN sign and gain the street. I make for the curb to signal the nearest vacant taxi, although it crosses my mind that maybe what I'd better send for would be an ambulance.

Then I glance with trepidation at my child. Escape from the store and fresh air have restored him to life. His pallor is fled, his fever abated, his weakness turned miraculously into buoyant energy.

"How do you feel?" I ask with concern.

"Swell," comes the outrageous answer. "Say, Mum, how about taking me to a shooting gallery?"

"No!" This is one time I am firm. "Very regrettable accidents have occurred sometimes at shooting galleries."

THE BIG
INFLAMMABLES

THE BIG INFLAMMABLES

THE way summer hotels are run in this country is amazing. What's yet more amazing is that Americans, pampered in modern comfort and Statler efficiency, continue to patronize them. Perched on our rock-bound coast from Rhode Island to the Border are a string of large wooden hostelries which are highly expensive and highly inflammable and which in atmosphere and equipment remain definitely pre-war. (I refer to the Cuban.) The only advancement is in rates. At the same price for which at an average city hotel you could get a sitting-room, bedroom and bath, not to mention such further amenities as running ice water, a radio and a few tasty French prints, you are grudgingly allotted a little cell somewhere up under the eaves that reminds you of your quarters at boarding school before you put up the pennants and the Harrison Fishers. The floor is bare except for a flighty rag rug that has a prankish way of humping itself against any door you're trying to open. The room is furnished in best Battle Creek sanitarium style, which may explain why some people find these places restful. The bed is white painted iron, caparisoned with a white hospital spread and at the foot an extra blanket—a good deal like the one Junior just took to camp. There is a mail-order bureau with drawers that stick and, if you're lucky, a "chiffonier" with more drawers that stick, an armchair and a golden oak rocker with a bit of dish towelling tied demurely to its back. There is generally no trace of a desk so any necessary correspondence must be done either on the lap or at a small wicker table that is intended to hold a pitcher and glasses and that exhibits a strong tendency to bend at the knees. The closet (which is sometimes an old fashioned wardrobe and sometimes a series of hooks behind chintz curtains) can contain only a minimum of clothing. Coats and bathrobes have perforce to hang decoratively on the backs of doors. The bathroom (if indeed you get one) is in the same style of Wesleyan simplicity. The tub like an ancient sycamore is starting to shed its enamel; the basin is the diminutive size of a drinking fountain, and the whats-is is the dear old kind that works (or doesn't) from a high overhanging box. There being but one small shelf for all toiletries, the overflow of bottles has to go on the window ledge and get occasionally rained in on. Sometimes there is a sort of transom between your bathroom and that of the couple next door, which is cozy unless the man is a hearty who whistles when he shaves, in which case the hurling of missiles through the aperture is permissible.

The circulation of air in the bedroom is negligible and you mention the fact to the bell-boy who shows you these accommodations. He explains that all you need to do is open the door into the hall, privacy being supposedly insured by a flimsy curtain that has a way of whipping to and fro like Old Glory, revealing tantalizing flashes to stray passers-by, all of whom are prone to goof.

The bell-boy is the chatty sort whom the old ladies think will go far, although it's your private opinion that it may be to a premature death. He tells you that this is one of the best rooms in the house and you'd better enjoy it while you can because a lady from Hingham has had it for fifteen years and as she arrives in three days, they'll have to move you. This is nothing out of the way. People are constantly being moved. Tramping the corridors are hourly lines of chambermaids, bell-boys and dislodged guests, bearing armloads of apparel from one room to another. Not that there's very much difference in the rooms.

The hotel is American plan, meals being at strictly specified hours. Breakfast is over at 9:30 and if you wake up at ten, the only place for coffee is the local dog-wagon. The dining-room is a vast, barren affair presided over by a terribly refined lady head-waiter. One wonders whether or not to call her "Captain." She smiles but doesn't mean it, looks you over and allots you a table several acres away. The bare floor is of a peculiarly resounding type of wood. The old habitués, already seated, stop talking and eating to inspect the entrance of new arrivals, apparently expecting them to throw bombs. In an attempt to become invisible you find yourself tip-toeing. A menu is handed you and as you start to say what you want, you are reproachfully handed a pencil and slip and told that guests must write out their own orders. This gives rise to the slight complication of wondering just what to put down, the items on the menu being presented in somewhat verbose style. For example, "Fresh killed young tender roast Vermont turkey" won't all

go on one line and yet to write merely "Turkey" seems
as inadequate as writing just plain "beans" for "Green
garden pride-of-Maine buttered beans." Another thing
about writing your own slip, no matter how modest
a meal you order, by the time you've begun with
"Queen olives" and "Crisp celery" and ended with
"Cookies," sometimes known as "Friandises," giving
a line to each item, the list looks like something for
Lucullus. However, when it arrives the feast is delicate
enough, the scantiness of the portions being accentu-
ated by the curious custom of serving all vegetables in
individual canary-baths.

The young lady who waits on your table is a nice
girl who's working her way through Normal School
and who, after the first meal, tells you all about her
mother. The bus-boy who brings up a hot tray filled
with cold corn-bread turns out to be a theological
student with what he calls a broad point of view. He
follows the chatty employee tradition, too. He's apt to
ask you if you've read "The Grapes of Wrath" and if
you know Hedy Lamarr and you suspect that given a
little encouragement he might try to sell you Dr.
Buchman. As the waitresses and bell-boys sooner or
later all turn up on the beach, it's well to memorize
what they look like so you won't cut them dead and
get a name for being "stuck-up."

Social life in one of the big inflammables follows a curious pattern of its own. There is sometimes a "hostess" who wanders about the lobby and asks if she can do anything for you. For one who invariably replies "Good God, no!" it is difficult to say for certain just what her duties are, but she apparently helps people get together, and from the looks of the people that's O.K., too. There is a formula for summer hotel clientèle; a few energetic families who go out splendidly for brine and sunburn and appear only at meals in the last stages of health; a number of young girls trying hard to pretend they don't know their mothers; and a few transient, highly irritable motorists. There are few young people and the only extra man is a gay buck with dyed hair who goes around trying to look as if he'd just played five sets of tennis, although he's never to be seen on the courts and who always tells the waitress at lunch that he'll be out for dinner. There is a glamour girl who dashes in and out to change from shorts to slacks and then back to shorts again, also a few small children who run through rooms in chronic states of smothered giggles. The rest are a varied and interesting collection of fossils who, like the swallows, return year after year. After breakfast and lunch they sit on the porch and stare. After dinner they sit in the lounge and continue to stare. A few play cards, some find diversion at the desk complaining to the management or fine-combing the hotel register and some inspect for the twentieth time the merchandise of the Armenian who sells linen, kimonos and maple sugar at the end of the lobby. Sometimes entertainment is furnished by a quartette of lady musicians or a chance performance of a strolling puppet show. In the evenings the women wear little printed chiffon numbers, neither short nor long, that are not dinner and not daytime dresses, a variety of garment seen only at summer hotels, unless possibly at garden parties in Liverpool.

I am doubtless blind to the charm of this colorful aspect of the American scene. Whatever its appeal to the more appreciative, I still claim it's a hell of a price to pay for atmosphere.

IN QUEST
OF TEA

IN QUEST OF TEA

I AM about to offer a prize to the first hotel in this country that will give me a cup of tea. It needn't be a particularly wonderful cup nor do I ask for any particular variety. It just has to be tea. I happen not to belong to the Brotherhood of Great American Coffee Drinkers and while it may seem an anglophile affectation like saying shed-ule to prefer tea, I not only prefer it, I crave it. I ought to give up and force myself into becoming an Ovaltine addict, because after years of harsh experience one comes to realize that to expect any hotel to understand the first thing about that excellent brew is a sheer case of arrested development.

The process of ordering tea from one's room in every United States hostelry is so similar, one wonders if it isn't set down in some book of rules gotten up by the inn-keepers' union. You pick up the phone, get the Room Service and quite simply, and in what you consider to be impeccable diction, state the fact that you would like some tea.

"I beg your pardon, what was that?" comes the invariable response.

"Tea," you reply.

"What was that you wanted?" asks Room Service with the good-humored indulgence one extends to a child.

"Tea," you repeat patiently and wait a full minute for indications of enlightenment from the other end of the wire.

"I didn't quite get that," says Room Service, a legendary sort of being who, like an Oriental deity, is sometimes male and sometimes female.

"Tea," you shout, wondering if there's any way of pronouncing it differently.

Room Service has by now discarded any pretense of any attitude of respect and comes back with a loud and rather irritable "WHAT?"

"Tea!" you wail. "Hot tea! T! T for Thomas!"

Room Service still unconvinced snaps "Spell it."
"T-E-A!"

"Oh, *tea!*" says Room Service in the relieved tone
of someone finally making out the words of a for-
eigner struggling with an English dictionary. Then
adds in a voice of incredulity, "Did you say tea!"—
implying there may be a catch somewhere and you're
about to come back with "April Fool!"

"Yes, tea," you gasp and Room Service says, "Oh,"
which may mean anything.

There is a pause. Room Service appears to be pon-
dering the strangeness of this request. You wonder
if asking for a deck of heroin might not be simpler.
After weighing the situation for an appreciable time
Room Service comes forth with,

"What kind of tea was that you wanted?"

You are tempted to say, "make it pink and Cam-
bric" but you control yourself enough to say Orange
Pekoe or whatever.

Room Service then raises the question, which in
my particular case causes most of the difficulty, by
asking if I want cream or lemon. I am an eccentric
of the old school who likes milk in tea, a taste that
in this country is looked upon with as much amaze-
ment as a liking for bird's nest soup. However, by
nature an optimist, I come forth bravely with:

"Neither; I'd like milk."

"Did you wish cream or lemon?" comes the annoying refrain.

"I want *milk*," I state with what I consider admirable forebearance.

"Did you wish a bottle of milk in addition to the tea?"

"No," I say, pushing down a gorge that is rising, "I just want milk in my tea."

"Did you wish the milk put in the tea?"

"No." I manage to say, blinking back my tears," I want it in a little pitcher. The same as a cream pitcher. But I don't like cream in tea. I hate cream in tea! I like milk."

This appears to be slightly taxing to the delicate mentality of Room Service for there generally follows a long silence. You begin to fear Room Service may have fainted and in more gentle tones inquire: "Did you get that?" Room Service now seemingly very far away, says, "Yes, Ma'am" and hangs up. You sigh with relief and settle down to a book or the evening paper. The phone rings and you answer it. A voice totally unlike the one with which you've just been conferring, says it begs your pardon but it's Room Service and was that tea you wanted? By this time the word "tea" has begun to take on that eerie, other-world sound that comes with repetition and you find yourself doubting if after all it really is tea that you mean. However, you brave it out and say, "Yes, tea," adding, if you're in my category, "with milk" in the same hopeless tone in which you might say "with rubies." You hang up and wait.

Eventually there is a knock at the door and a waiter appears, panting (all waiters seem to pant) and bearing a tray laden with an array of that gleaming alloy of which hotel silver and souvenirs of the Empire State Building are apparently composed. The waiter accepts his tip with a flourish and departs, and you turn to inspect what he has brought. Besides a tea-pot, water-jug, cream-pitcher and two kinds of sugar bowls (one mysteriously enough is filled with confectioner's sugar) there is an interest-

ing collection of spoons and sometimes a knife or
fork thrown in for good luck. Often there will be
both cream and lemon, the latter being a fossil-like
specimen bearing the blackened evidence of having
been cut with a steel knife. In the case of us unfortunate milk-fanciers, if we're lucky enough to get
milk, it arrives in a special much larger receptable.
Sometimes they send a quart bottle and I've more
than once been the recipient of a pitcher of it boiling
hot. Perhaps it would be simpler if instead of asking for milk we bellowed lustily for rum.

I hope whoever is responsible for defiling that
noble herb by tying it up in little cotton bags, dunk-
ing the bags in tepid water and having the effrontery
to call this seepage tea is doing eternal penance,
writhing in an endless pit of old coffee-grounds. To
a tea-lover this is the equivalent of serving Orange-
Crush to a wine connoisseur. Gingerly you raise the
lid of the pot, hoping against all reason to behold a
simple and delicious brew with a sturdy deposit of
tea-leaves at the bottom, only to be shocked by the
sight of a nasty little object that looks like the sort
of thing you're afraid the surgeon may have left in
your appendix wound. This floats on the surface of
the not any too hot water exuding an aura of dark
brown coloring matter which, with the aid of a little

stirring, eventually permeates the liquid like Tin-tex. Attached to this unpleasant tampon by a string is a bit of cardboard that shamelessly proclaims the name of the merchant responsible for this horror. When the lid is lifted it all slips down into the pot and the taste of cardboard, string and printed matter are added to the blend. A few flecks of lint from the bag float dreamily about on the surface and help further to disguise the fact that what you're drinking is intended to be tea. Meekly you fish out the label, hang it to dry on the outside of the pot and pour yourself a cup.

The pot holds just about one cupful and with misplaced optimism you pour some of the hot water over the soggy tampon with the vague delusion that it's good for another go. The first pouring has had a remote resemblance to tea and has not been as bad as you'd anticipated. The second cup, however, is just a sort of second rinsing of tan-bark and if you're crack-brained enough to attempt a third, the result is filtered water.

Maybe I'm just an old fuss button. For undoubtedly thousands of Americans unquestioningly accept and down this insipid beverage and as far as I know there's never been any petition presented at Washington in protest. I guess the only thing for me to do

outside my own house is to patronize Gipsy tea-
rooms where, in order to have the solace of behold-
ing tea-leaves in my cup, I shall have the further
advantage of getting my fortune told in them.

GREAT GUNS

GREAT GUNS

THE duck season is going full tilt and I guess all those hardy Nimrods who are out quaking away happily in gale-swept blinds and little boats that leak ice-water are having a high old time. Duck shooting (or, if one would be a purist about these things . . . "shootin' ") must certainly be a lot of fun for those who think it's fun.

Once in what is known as a blue moon, through some mistake I get asked to go duck-shooting and through some even greater mistake I hear myself saying I'll go. It's practically impossible to say NO to sportsmen. They have a way of extending invitations to accompany them on one of their specialized outings in the manner of issuing a royal command. A chance to go ice-boating beagling, pig-sticking . . . what have you . . . is proffered with all the solemnity of offering you an honorary degree . . . the golden opportunity of a life-time which none but the most abject cretin would pass up. And I who in a National Sap Contest would qualify for "Miss America" invariably fall for it. Some day I'll find myself sitting in a cage while a trainer takes on a raw bunch of Bengal tigers. The moment after I've accepted I realize it's a serious mistake. I explain that I don't know how to shoot. That only encourages the prospective host who says, "Then you can watch me," to which I can only bleat that that'll be dandy. Then, remembering my scanty wardrobe in which my only concessions to sport are a tweed suit, a pair of golf shoes and an old mink coat, I protest that I haven't any suitable clothes.

"You've surely got duck-pants?" comes the incredulous inquiry.

"No duck-pants, nor pheasant-pants . . . in fact no pants at all." An admission that considerably shocks your honest hunter.

"Haven't you any old waders?"

"Old waders?"

"You know . . . old hip boots."

Shooting togs, like brandy, must be old it seems. I have visions of trying to wedge several yards of rubber boots into my hall closet which has just room for the vacuum cleaner and one pair of galoshes.

"No, I haven't any old waders," I say, suppressing an impulse to add, "And I haven't any old divers' suits kicking about, either."

"How about some old mackinaws, leather jackets and wind-breakers?" He might as well say, "How about some old halberds, breast-plates and cuirasses?" The only ancient and heavy garment of a sporting nature in my possession is a leftover from college days; a gem that once belonged to my roommate bearing the legend "Varsity" in yellow letters across the front, or back (the article is quite sexless). And that's enough to send any duck back to Hudson's Bay.

Lack of equipment, however, doesn't let one off. People who shoot ducks always have a lot of extra apparel which they insist upon lending you . . . rare old items in which they take an antiquarian's pride. They have worn them every season for years, it seems, and doubtless their fathers before them. I'm not much for wearing other people's clothes, much less shooting clothes which, even when clean, give forth an impression of having been hung for some time in the game-room. Moreover there's always the

element of shock as to what you may find in the pocket
. . . anything from a briar pipe to a hardened mitten
and an old Chiclet. The true sportsman, however,
lends them in the manner of Prince Charming giving
his cloak to the Little Match Girl and I haven't the
courage to refuse.

Subsequently, some days later I find myself setting
forth with a heavy bag and an even heavier heart for
shore points and for what some might call a "shooting-
box" but what looks pretty much like just a house
to me. The company is agreeable even if it's hard to
understand their lingo and the evening is pleasant
. . . too pleasant for anyone who has to get up at four
the following morning. All splendid sports must, it
seems, start at a zero hour. Someone wakes you . . .
someone far too cheerful and for a desperate minute
or two you lie there trying to figure out where you are.
Not that after you've done the figuring you're any
happier. It's still pitch dark outside and to judge by the
temperature of the room a second Glacier Age has
begun. The individual who woke you closes your window and if there's a fire-place starts a fire that merely
smokes dolefully and doesn't get really going till
you're dressed and on your chattering way. I generally make an attempt to de-frost my undergarments
by taking them into bed and lying on them for a time

but this is of little help and the inevitable moment arrives when, with the bravura of those Atlantic City exhibitionists who go for a dip on New Year's Day, I stand naked in a frigid room and pull over my quaking limbs a congealed suit of what is aptly known as "heavies." If any gal reaches a state of worldly vanity when she fancies herself a potential Du Barry, all she need do to bring herself back to penitence, is to behold her form divine encased from wrist to ankle in a gray woolen union suit. Small wonder the Mormons use them as their symbol for the "Garment of Humility." What goes on top doesn't help much either. The shirt is a veteran number that saw service at the Mexican border and from the feel of it still has bits of cactus in it. The pants are dark green and look as if they'd been whipped together out of the hall runner. To make them more practical they have a copious *derrière* that hangs down in a sort of saddle-bag effect. What goes on the feet (what doesn't go on them?) is also seductive . . . two pairs of socks several sizes too large, some fleece-lined Eskimo booties known as "shoe-packs" and over all this a pair of rubber boots with feet that a circus clown would itch to borrow. Then there are a few layers of sweaters, mackinaws and wind-breakers which form a fat straight-jacket and make you look like a penguin. All this elaborate casing works on the principle of a thermos jar maintaining the creature within either at scalding or at freezing temperatures.

As if the sight of myself in this outfit weren't already sufficiently unappetizing, I find I'm expected to rally round a kitchen table with a lot of hearties and try to down a rugged mess of coffee, ham and eggs which at this bleak hour gets no further than my craw. Everybody seems horribly awake. There is a good deal of lusty talk among the hunters. The moment some people get into rough sporting clothes they talk in tones several degrees louder than ordinary and all final "g's" fall like leaves in autumn. They also drink their coffee vocally which probably gets them in the mood. After the repast they start making ready, stamping their feet quite a lot and doing alarming things with their guns, clicking triggers, loading them and practicing their aim all too frequently in my direction. Someone pairs off the party telling them where they're to go. I keep hoping they'll forget me but eventually I am relegated to some poor wretch and we set forth.

Once outdoors things seem better. There's something about being out before dawn in late November or early December that makes you feel you're doing something big for your country. I look brave and splendid and start doing deep-breathing exercises. A truck takes us to some unknown destination and we start walking to the blind, a process which owing to that footgear requires a new technique that practically necessitates doing the splits. Lurching along over rough ground and dragging through reed-strewn water takes on the quality of the familiar nightmare when you're trying to escape an oncoming locomotive and your legs have suddenly turned into unpulled molasses candy. Finally we reach a little wooden structure sitting forlornly in the middle of a marsh as if left there by a flood. This is the blind . . . our happy home for the rest of the day. Climbing into a blind in all this excess attire is a humiliating ma- noeuvre that involves a good deal of struggling and puffing. Each mammoth boot has to be helped over the top, hoisting it by hand, while the escort hoists the rest of me from the rear . . . also by hand. Somehow we get in and then the fun begins.

People who shoot well tell you there's nothing like sitting out in a blind all day and they're right. One remains cooped up from before dawn till after sunset with one or possibly two hunters, some sinister pieces of firearms and a very damp dog in a pen the size of a sawed-in-half sentry box. The only place to recline is on a narrow plank, there's no space in which to

move about and all the time little knife-like drafts
play viciously upon your most vulnerable parts. The
novelty of it all makes things start off well enough.
You even think it's going to be fun. The dawn breaks
and ducks rise off the water and your companion
shoots one or two or not as the case may be. Then
begins the long experience of gradually freezing into
insensibility. Hunters must keep warm through excitement, or if they do get cold they like it. It makes
them feel more like hunters. The dogs manage to
keep alive by shivering very violently while as for
that hot-house excrement of over-civilization, myself,
I begin to realize how an artichoke must feel while
being put through the Bird's-Eye process of refrigera-
tion. There's no possible way of keeping warm. You
can't run briskly up and down a space the size of a
witness-box, you don't even dare beat your arms across
your chest for fear of hitting one of your companions
in the eye . . . not that now and then you don't entertain the impulse. All you can do is sit there waiting
for that supposed moment when death from freezing
becomes rather pleasant. I try to endure it all with
fortitude. I think hard of noble souls like Admiral
Byrd down in his polar shack and St. Bernards out on
the Matterhorn, but they don't warm me up. I try
to rise above it and indulge in bright conversation but

hunters aren't much for repartee when they're on the job. I try hugging the retriever who by now has had a few dips in the water and is covered with tiny icicles. Sometimes it rains and that's considered fun, too. It trickles down my neck, seeps along my rear and runs playfully off the end of my nose. I console myself, remembering how good rain is for the complexion, then think what's the use of a good complexion when you're about to die of pneumonia.

Your true hunter becomes so absorbed in the joys of the game he frequently forgets about lunch, but I don't. I sit there dreaming about hot soup and steaming roasts until someone pacifies me with a soggy sandwich and a chunk of bitter chocolate which I devour along with some tasty bits of mitten.

And, meanwhile, what of the ducks? The first few of the morning have fled and only a few stray ones come in . . . not that I ever get a chance to see them. Whenever a good flight comes near someone always hisses, "Get down, get down! Don't move! Don't look up!" and I have yet to behold these fabulous birds in any state other than dead or flapping their last on the water . . . neither of which is much fun. I am not of the race of heroes and the sight of bloodshed fails to elate me. Furthermore, there's one thing I invariably forget until I'm out in a blind and there's no retreat, that is my deathly fear of guns. I don't even like to pass in front of the cannons of a Civil War Memorial. I'm even afraid of those paper crackers and I have never been known to get the plot of a mystery play because I sit with my fingers in my ears throughout the entire performance. I do the same in a duck-blind and by the end of the day my hands are devoid of circulation.

It all eventually comes to an end and by some miracle I don't die of pneumonia, which is rather disappointing. The party breaks up and I am sent home with a couple (or maybe it's a brace) of ducks. The irony of this is . . . and here goes for a heinous admission . . . I don't really like wild duck. I try to. I follow all instructions concerning their proper treatment and cooking. I hang them outside the window till the neighbors complain and buzzards start coming up from the south. I have them cooked the stipulated brief time . . . in fact my cook has been trained so thoroughly, practically all she does is show them to the stove . . . and I still don't like them. There's a vague sugestion of cod liver oil about the best of them that I find distressing and I'm not good at carving them. Moreover I have a molar that acts like a magnet for shot and I am as averse to chewing shot as I am to spewing it forth.

GREAT GUNS

I guess the thing for me to do is to stay home and eat broiled chicken. And that'll probably be OK by the hunters too.

SHOP

TALK

LONG LIVE THE STICKS!

NOT long ago I had the dubious pleasure of conversing for a few minutes with a well-upholstered Park Avenue matron, one of those caryatids of American society who know as much about America as I do about Thibet. To her anything west of the Alleghenies is just so much Flatbush and all true civilization is bounded by Bailey's Beach, Aiken and the Everglades Club. Someone told her I had just returned from a tour of the Middle West and after being politely assured that no, I had not been out attending Junior League conferences nor yet organizing the Republican women, merely acting, she asked me a few routine questions about what she jocosely called "the Hinterland" in the manner of someone questioning a welfare worker concerning life in Hell's Kitchen. Something in my defiantly enthusiastic defense of the Tank Towns gave her food for thought (if I don't overestimate the process) and with superb magnanimity she announced: "I do think we Easterners are awfully narrow at times. Why I'm told that Kansas City has an excellent museum and I myself have met some really charming people from Michigan." I assured her that good museums and charming people were to be found not only in Kansas City and Michigan, but in Ohio and Wisconsin, Indiana and the Dakotas, to which she said, "Oh, really?" only because she was too refined to say, "Oh, yeah?" and walked away without waiting to hear that not only can I stand it, I thrive on it. I watched her retreating figure (I refer to distance), murmured, "There, but by the grace," and at the same time thanked fate for the job that for ten years has given me the opportunity to travel from one end to the other of this country, to get to know it and in consequence to become what is vulgarly known as a "push-over" for it.

My viewpoint is based purely upon a somewhat

superficial familiarity with audiences, auditoriums, hotels, and occasionally the houses . . . or more often the "homes" . . . of some of the local citizens. However, I've seen sufficient to realize that touring the "Sticks," despite the contention of some that that word should be spelled "Styx," can be pleasurable, colorful and even at times adventuresome. And for the actor who refuses ever to stir from Broadway, I feel not so much contempt as pity.

Persons on the order of that Park Avenue lady frequently ask, "But what sort of audiences do you get?" as if they expected them to turn up in sunbonnets and coon-skin caps. The easiest reply is that the average out-of-town audience differs from the average New York variety only in that it's usually a lot better. By that I mean better to play to and better mannered. In these places a legitimate theatrical performance is something to anticipate for weeks in advance, to attend with respect and (if it merits it) to appreciate with enjoyment. No wonder actors can give their best before such houses! To begin with, the audience arrives on time and in a state of sobriety. Parties of jaded playgoers don't straggle in late to wedge themselves into distant seats, trampling all over such as have had the decency and taste to arrive on time. Nor are they more interested in who's in the audience than who's on the stage. Nor, just before the final curtain, do they start squirming into coats and wraps and making hundred yard dashes up the aisles for the nearest exit and the first taxi. They sit through the show with interest and considerate behavior and if they've enjoyed themselves are generous enough to let the actors know about it. All this does not signify that the small-town audience is in any way naïve. They are, on the whole, quite discriminating and know their literary and artistic onions quite as well as their metropolitan neighbors. Theirs is the blessed advantage of having time to "keep up with things," as they themselves might put it, and I am constantly amazed and not infrequently discomfited to discover that these people, even at long range, are a deal more alert and *au courant* than I. They read the standard best sellers and have time, too, for the classics; they hear the best of the traveling lecturers; they glean what treasures the radio has to offer and they even follow the columnists with fidelity and can tell you, if you feel you must know, what Dietrich wore to the last opening at Grauman's and who took Brenda Frazier to the Stork Club last Friday. They have, in short, all the mental equipment of the New York playgoer minus his infinite capacity for being bored; and speaking from the other side of the footlights, for attention, response and enthusiasm I'll stake Ypsilanti, Sioux City or Chickasaw anytime against the Martin Beck sold out at twenty dollars top for the Greater Babies' Milk Fund.

One hears on the road from time to time a curious half-boastful, half-apologetic confession . . . "You know we are notorious for being a cold audience." This is an interesting fallacy. Audiences do not vary regionally. They are mercurial aggregations and in the same town on two nights running you may have a splendid house one evening that makes you think Bernhardt couldn't have been so good after all, and the next, one of those frozen, sit-on-their-hands sort that almost persuades you to abandon the theatre and take refuge in a silent Trappist order. My particular specialty of solo work permits me to rush in where large productions fear to tread. The result is that I've come in contact with every variety of gathering from the boiled-shirt splendor of the fashionable benefit, through the warm response of the college groups even on to the cozy get-together of the State Penitentiary. I am called upon to entertain (or such is my fond hope) universities, clubs, charitable organizations and those subscription courses that bring culture to the town in the way of lecturers, musicians and myself thrown in as a bit of lighter superfluity. Of course, the best of audiences is still that of the regular theatre, when it's good. Of the specialized groups I find myself happiest when performing in the large co-educational universities. These audiences are alert, discriminating and wonderfully enthusiastic and the slight tempering of just enough of the academic, is a challenge to do one's best. Groups of all-men or of all-women are seldom satisfactory. Sex, it seems, must rear its pretty head even when it comes to these matters. However, an all-man audience is a good deal better than an all-woman and I'm safe in saying that the very worst of audiences is the sort of woman's club where middle-aged women grow more and more cultured and less and less amused, where applause is heard through kid gloves darkly and laughter is confined to an occasional "Tsk! Tsk!" The next worst audience is a school of young girls under college age. They have a curious way of reacting in shrill squeals and when a number of them are gathered together the effect is that of playing to a group of steam sirens. The subscription course aggregation varies but generally speaking is very good. Of course, it can at times be stiff and apathetic and every so often one becomes subtly aware of the presence of those sour or irate husbands whose wives have dragged them there against their wills. But usually you can count on a pleasant evening. In the case of these groups, one runs up against the "word of introduction" custom which can be tedious and at times diverting. At a university in California a professor made me feel at home by telling the assembly he didn't quite know how to introduce me as up to then they'd had "things of a cultural nature." And among my better souvenirs is the memory of the New England chairman who stated with yankee brevity that "owing to the high price of Rear-Admiral Byrd we have Miss Skinner with us this evening." In two places . . . one a revivalist college and the other a ladies' uplift organization . . . I lived through the harrowing experience of having the evening's entertainment open with a long and fervent prayer and in a certain Ohio steel town the lady running the program who, incidentally, also ran a school for the feeble-minded, marched after me onto the stage and sat herself down comfortably in one of the chairs I use in my act, her reason being that "members might like to ask questions."

The auditoriums differ as contrastingly as the audiences that fill them . . . or don't as the case may be. One plays in regulation theatres that in show language are known as "legitimate" and movie palaces that might be considered as born out of wedlock, in tumbled-down "Oprey Houses" and armories, on high-school stages and perilous platforms erected in hotel ballrooms (some of these latter even have casters which make them roll about and add to the fun). I frequently appear in churches and synagogues. In one Illinois house of worship I found myself hemmed in by a choir-railing that came to my waist and when I sat down, as I must in some of my numbers, only my head and shoulders were visible. I have acted, or rather shouted, in a roller-skating rink and once had to make my way in Tarzan fashion through the palms and azaleas of a mammoth greenhouse.

When it comes to dressing rooms, I've made up in cellars, organ-lofts, gymnasiums, locker rooms and lavatories. I recall a certain swank Florida club equipped with everything but a place for the use of visiting performers where I made my changes on a roof and I can still shudder at the recollection of the Mississippi hamlet where in order to make up, I stood on a board laid across two chairs to avoid a sewer main that had burst. Once, when delayed by a train wreck and having to dash from Boston out to Wellesley, I managed to change from traveling suit to evening dress in a taxi, thereby causing the driver a nasty shock. In some places, dressing rooms are neat and clean, in others you are led to believe the local people must think you're going to give them scenes from "Tobacco Road." Some are even inhabited. I've had interesting encounters with cockroaches, bats (many old theatres harbor whole flocks of these) and scorpions, and in the Rio Grande country even an opossum strayed in to inspect the make-up.

One meets, of course, many people and while there's scant time for becoming deeply acquainted, one learns their salient qualities. They are alert and energetic, intelligent and keen to "keep up." They are very kind and extremely hospitable (at times too much so) and above all they have a zest and a healthy enjoyment of life that is pleasantly contagious. They can be somewhat overwhelming when it comes to entertaining the visiting lion and one rather wishes they'd concentrate on the true meaning of this word and realize that large teas and receptions do not come under such a heading. Meeting masses of prominent citizens and being fed a cup of coffee and a lady finger is hardly going to rejoice the performer who is longing for an arm-

chair, some substantial food and drink and a few
congenial souls with whom to relax. However, there
are many who understand such amenities and I
look back with delight on the good times I've had in
Ottumwa, Iowa, Kingsville, Tex., Beliot, Wis., and
Delaware, O., to name only a few.

The road can even offer adventure of sorts. I've
sat up all night on a train that crawled through the
Arkansas floods, wheels completely under water, no
one knowing if the rails were still intact; I've choked
my way through a "duster" in the Panhandle and

(if the Los Angeles Chamber of Commerce will allow me to mention such things) have become acquainted with earthquakes and landslides. Nor is one's part always a passive one. I've helped a Wisconsin station-master shovel snow off the tracks at a God-forsaken junction when the train was so late we were arranging for a Swedish farm woman to take us in for the night. In North Carolina I had to make one very long jump by taxi, the driver of which, a mountaineer, not only didn't know the roads but hadn't the remotest idea of how to drive; in addition to which he'd bolstered up his nerve with a powerful dose of corn liquor. After a few near collisions and an unfortunate detour into a cotton field, I persuaded him to take the back seat and have a nap while I drove the rattle-trap vehicle seventy-five miles over the mountains. In a town in Tennessee I descended from the train expecting to be met by the ladies of the organization that was "having me" there, only to be greeted by an untethered and enraged bull. As far as any experiences that might be termed "sinister" are concerned, they are negligible, and for the benefit of those who believe that civilization begins east of Harrisburg, I should like to state that the only place I ever experienced a hold-up was in Boston.

Then, too, trooping gives one a pretty fair knowledge of the country. It's a never diminishing emotion to see from the train window the boiling brown waters of the Missouri, the bright undulating wheat fields of Iowa, the prairie lands of Kansas that gradually crack and heave into the jagged foothills of the Rockies, the awesome stretches of the Great Salt Lake, the mountains of Oregon with their fairy-tale forests, the vivid soil of Oklahoma oozing oil. One might continue *ad nauseam*. When I'm the oldest living inmate of the Actor's Home, I'll have a good many memories to keep me entertained. I'll remember crossing the Mississippi at Baton Rouge and watching the river fog drifting across the bow of the paddle-wheel ferry; I'll see again the beauty of the huge rotary snow-plough whirling the drifts from the Minnesota tracks and hear the panting of the giant engines bearded with icicles in the early morning cold of the Great Northern station. There will be pictures of things like the white herons fluttering up from the Florida bayous, the blue-bonnets that transform the Texas plain into a gay tapestry rug, the V-shaped flocks of geese flying south along the great rivers. It's a picturesque and beautiful land and no one knows it better than the actor who goes on tour with his eyes open. It's a good life, this barnstorming one. I shall always continue to say "Long Live the Sticks!"

"I SAW YOUR FATHER
IN 'KISMET'"

"I SAW YOUR FATHER IN 'KISMET'"

IT is a lamentable fact that actors on being met by the public for the first time are frequently accused of being distrait and even (a far worse term of opprobrium) "high hat!" This fallacy . . . and I'm a loyal enough Lodge member to maintain that it *is* a fallacy . . . is due largely to the fact that actors are simple souls who don't know any better than to get themselves involved in those gruesome gatherings, sometimes social, sometimes for charity, usually overcrowded, and always terrible when they are "being met!" Nobody, not even a candidate running for public office, is much good on such occasions and actors who often as not are retiring by nature and desperately ill at ease in any milieu other than the theatre, show up worse than most celebrities because they're expected to be so much better. They are bored and unhappy and their attempts to hide this ennui results in that "high hat" expression. They shake hands with swarms of people they say they're glad to meet when they're anything but; then when they've managed to hook up with some kindred spirit and are beginning to enjoy themselves, someone comes up with another someone "they just have to meet" and they do just have to. It all makes for bad feeling on the part of both the professionals and the well-meaning but misguided public. One should abide by the Charles Frohman principle that "actors should be heard and seen but never met!"

The root of most of the trouble lies in the fact that one is constantly being overwhelmed with remarks to which there is absolutely no reply. When average individual meets average individual, he or she generally tries to start the conversational ball rolling, shoving it along with certain polite, if trite, utterances that will enable the other person to respond with further shoves. When the same individuals, however, meet players they seem to labor under the illusion that they must greet them with something special and the greeting turns out to be so exceptionally special it leaves the actor high and dry. This is too bad because certain starry-eyed devotees of the theatre still believe all Thespians are brilliant creatures of wit and repartee. Well, even if they were, nobody upon meeting them gives them half a chance. It's like expecting one to exchange sparkling badinage with a sand bunker. For instance some bustling member of the sandwich committee will lead a beaming fellow member up to the captive lion saying, "Miss Jones, do you know Miss Barrymore?" Whereat Miss Jones, her beams by now becoming pure infra-red, gurgles, "I know Miss Barrymore of course but Miss Barrymore doesn't know me." Or, "I've seen you, Miss Barrymore, but you haven't seen me." And what in the name of dear kind Emily Post is Miss Barrymore to reply? "So what?" is obviously the answer but one can't jeopardize the box-office.

The actor lives and blossoms on praise and any who tells you it means nothing to him should be suspended from Equity. "I had a superb time at your show" or "I loved your performance" such phrases heaven knows are blessedly welcome and an easy pleasure to reply to. Without them we wither and pine away into character bits in the Federal Theatre. Occasionally, however . . . and maybe it's with an idea that we ought not to be pampered, someone will stand before us and in the tone of a prosecuting attorney, all but pointing an accusing finger, say "I saw you last year in Pittsburgh!" And nothing further. They don't follow the announcement with a reassuring "You were swell." They don't even say "You were terrible." They say just that and then stand waiting. What to reply? One can't say "Thank you" and "How nice" doesn't sound right somehow. "Oh" goes by unnoticed and "Did you?" merely brings forth a "Yes" after which they're still waiting for a rapid come-back. "I saw you once before" or "I'm coming to the matinee tomorrow" are similar stalemates. Then there are those discouraging comments to the effect that "I saw you years ago when I was just a tiny child" to which one could rally with 'Well, you don't look so darned young either" but one doesn't. Sometimes people launch forth into little excursions in autobiography. . . . "I remember seeing you because it was the first year I was married and my husband bought tickets to celebrate my having made my first cake" . . . very pretty indeed but there's still no answer to it.

Then there are the exclaimers to reckon with. These are the little women full of enthusiasm and good intentions who rush up, seize one's hand, forget to let it go and after gazing at one for what seems minutes with speechless rapture exclaim, "Well, well!" or "Oh, my dear, my dear!" or even just repeat one's name as if it were a priceless discovery like radium. And that's very bad indeed.

One non-replyable remark is constantly being made to me in particular. People tell me they've seen my father in "Kismet." This is very nice and I for one am always glad to hear it, but as my father played that play for three years to packed houses the length and breadth of the continent, the statement is not particularly staggering. "You'll be interested in meeting Miss Brown," a hostess will exclaim, her eyes dancing with suppressed excitement. "She has a special message for you" . . . as if it were a T. L. And Miss Brown's special message turns out to be that she too saw Father in "Kismet." This announcement is always made with such flourish, such an air of bringing glad tidings, it would be boorish indeed not to appear overwhelmed with happy surprise . . . to refrain from exclaiming "Not really!" in tones that imply "Great God, No!" Sometimes (and to be sure, it adds variety) they tell me they've seen my sire in plays he never even saw himself and nothing will persuade them that he never appeared in "The Garden of Allah" nor in "Omar the Tent Maker." One lady informed me that she laughed herself sick over Father's rendition of "Casey at the

Bat" and when I timidly suggested she must be thinking of DeWolf Hopper she grew indignant and practically told me I didn't know my own father. The best
policy, I find, is never to doubt their word. Especially
as they disbelieve not only me, sometimes they don't
even believe my father. To his politely firm "No, dear
lady, I did not play in 'The Man From Home' "
they've been known to protest, "But you must have
forgotten. Because I saw you in it." So why spoil their
fun?

Musicians and lecturers I daresay come in for these
opening remarks which are about as open as the Mor-
mon Temple. An author I know who lectures tells
me he finds himself pretty baffled when people say to
him, "I've got your book but I haven't read it yet."
Fond mothers are always bringing their children
around to meet great musicians because they're "starting piano"; and there's the story of the Philadelphia
débutante who, on being presented to Nansen, the
explorer, gasped, "Oh I'm so glad to meet you, Mr.
Nansen, because we keep a Swedish cook." Perhaps
it's a sort of panic or that curious state of awe that
for some reason overwhelms some people when they
find themselves in the presence of anyone whose name
appears in print. It's flattering if you like, but at the
same time a little trying to those same persons who, in

spite of the frequent publication of their names, are of perfectly standard clay and who, if given a chance, will react like any other human beings. The trouble is no one gives them even half a one.

FIRST NIGHTS

FIRST NIGHTS

THE big opening night is one of those phases of Gotham life that for some reason is listed under the heading of pleasure and why so many people season after season want to attend the nerve-wracking launching of a new play is as difficult to fathom as why any actors, authors and producers live through the ordeal. It is easy enough to see why the wretched members of the latter category anticipate these occasions with about as much enthusiasm as that with which any normal person might anticipate a major operation, but it is less easy to see why the first night hounds (and the word "hounds" is used advisedly) derive such apparent de-

light from being in at the kill. Going to opening
nights has become one of those activities known in-
comprehensively enough as "the thing to do" and
back in the gracious era of Frohman stars, Diamond
Jim Brady and stylish carriage trade it probably was.
The present opening night in taking on the quality
of the times has lost much of its elegance but is still
considered "brilliant." Well, maybe it is and by the
same token maybe that portion of the Easter parade
that gets jammed for a couple of hours in front of
St. Patrick's is brilliant, too. The congested mass
of humanity is pretty much the same and to the
claustrophobiac the sensation is equally acute and
one which neither a glimpse of Noel Coward in the
one case nor of Al Smith in the other can mitigate.
What, one presumes, makes for the brilliance of a
première is the presence of a goodly number of celebrities, pseudo-celebrities and celebrity starer-atters.
The celebrities have come chiefly to be seen, the
pseudos to bask in reflected glory and the starers
are there because they'd rather see Joan Crawford
in the flesh than an incarnation of Bernhardt, Ellen
Terry and Salvini on the stage. The play is definitely
not the thing on these occasions . . . it's the audience and to go to the theatre in order to see an
audience seems rather cockeyed.

Not that once in a while it isn't a lot of fun to find one's self part of a first night audience even if there is a definitely repetitious quality about that galaxy that makes one wonder sometimes if Elsa Maxwell isn't back of the whole thing. A little of it is highly entertaining and I for one can enjoy as keenly as any yahoo gazing at the itinerant Hollywood constellations, boops-a-daisying against favorite writers, gouging elbows into less favorite critics and sniffing the perfume of the current glamor débutante. It's exciting, it's gay, it makes you feel cosmopolitan. But I still don't think it's any way in which to go to see a play.

On these occasions it's as impossible to give a play one's absorbed attention as it is to study the paintings on Varnishing Day at a fashionable gallery. There are too many distractions. What's more, we put up with a vast amount of discomfort which, under any other circumstances we'd be writing letters to the *Times* about. Traffic within three blocks of the theatre is generally at a stand-still. One abandons one's taxi and hurries to the place on foot where one must battle one's way through crowds of curious onlookers in the street and of even more curious playgoers in the lobby. With the frenzy of a subway commuter one wedges one's way past the ticket taker, struggles to an aisle, fights for one's turn at an usher and finally reaches one's seat at the exact moment the show is scheduled to begin, only to be obliged to wait a half hour. For a "brilliant" New York opening always starts a good thirty minutes after the time it is announced for with the exception of those distinguished productions whose ad in the papers admonishes a boorish public that here is one performance that's going to start on time and nobody will be seated after 8:30, in which case the curtain can be counted upon to rise precisely at 8:45. This is definitely not the fault of the actors. They, poor devils, have been ready for hours and in a misery of impatience to get the agony over. It is simply because a New York audience won't arrive on time and the audience claims it's because no play ever starts on time and plays never start on time because managements know the audience won't arrive on time and there you are. Even when the public at long last gets to the theatre they don't go to their seats. The celebrities feel they must make an entrance and the starer-atters feel they must watch them and the remainder of the aggregation jam the lobby where they spend a lot of time greeting one another and telling each other how anxious they are to see this particular play. Outside of a few genuine theatre-lovers the only persons seated at the proper hour, and in consequence kept waiting, are critics with an early deadline. And that's no way to treat a critic either.

If the jam at the start of the evening has been bad, it's a sleety Monday at the World's Fair compared with the entr'acte crush. The entire audience goes out for a smoke . . . which means that a small portion of it gets out and the majority remain stuck in a hopeless and immovable huddle. A few who are sufficiently wise and agile to make an early dash, gain the pavement outside where they have comparative elbow room and are disturbed only by those peculiarly soiled boys who dart about spotting celebrities and asking them to write "To Butch" in greasy autograph books. Other less swift members of the audience (and their number is far too great) fight their way to the lobby where, adopting the attitude of the early American squatter, they refuse to budge. The remaining multitude spends half the intermission trying to reach the lobby or the smoking lounge and the next half trying to regain their seats. While from without, as if to pacify thwarted smokers caught in the backwash, great clouds of blue tobacco smoke waft back into the auditorium forming a haze that makes the actors in the ensuing scene look as if they were playing behind a transparency.

Similar turmoil arises during the next intermission and again at the finale, only then it's not quite so acute due to the fact that a good many people, foreseeing the conclusion of the play and desirous of grabbing the first taxis, have followed that good old American tradition of struggling into hats and coats and tramping heavily out on the final speech.

All this may be hectic, amusing, and, if you insist "brilliant." A play has to open and I suppose the idea back of it all is that it should be a gala occasion with friends of cast and management on hand to give it a great send-off. But the birth of a play for those concerned is a harrowing experience and there is something about this ultra-smart, self-absorbed audience that recalls those fashionable and heartless get-togethers at Versailles on the occasion of the queen's "accouchements." It was all very jolly for the spectators but a bit tough on the queen.

Plays have not only to open, they have, for some ghoulish reason, to be reviewed, and so we have critics. It seems a pity, incidentally, that the critics should be forced to come see a play under any but the most favorable auspices. The distracting presence of all these notables, nonentities and friends of the management must be anything but conducive to a mood of true playgoing. Moreover, it is doubtful if all the well-wishers in the world can, with their loyal applause, at all deter a critic from roasting a show if he believes it warrants it. Critics are not to be bought even if one producer going on the theory that none are infallible, arranges the seating of his first night audience in such a way that certain hand-picked friends are placed beside and around the more influential gentlemen of the press and in the manner of the opera claque at propitious moments they exchange loud and laudatory comments.

Another phase of the opening night that seems too bad is that fact of the late rising of the curtain. This means that almost every critic, in order to turn in his review, has to leave well before the finish. He can't see the thing through even if he'd like to. Not that he can't form an adequate opinion of what he has time to see but it would be nice if once in awhile they didn't have to miss most of the last act, or all. Moreover he is seeing a performance under conditions when the actors are in an agony of first night heebie-jeebies and certainly not at their best. Few actors worth their salt are any good on these occasions. Even so seasoned an artist as Sir Henry Irving is said to have given such inadequate opening exhibitions, reviewers were obliged to drop in later during the run to see what his performance was really like.

And what of the actor amid all this so-called "brilliance?" The poor wretch plays as secondary a part as the groom at a society wedding and is in an even worse state of collapse. He hears the hubbub outside and thinks, "Happy, happy people! They don't know." Peeking through the curtain he spots the critics and thinks, "They know . . . but they don't care." He wonders whatever made him want to be an actor . . . whatever makes him think he is. People come up to him, pat him on the back and say "Good luck" as if he were a test pilot about to take off in a condemned plane. He tries to think of his opening line and can't . . . of his closing line . . . that, too, eludes him. His throat is dry, his heart pounding itself into a rapid angina and his hands like aspens in a gale. It's a replica of an actor's nightmare only worse because in the typical actor's nightmare things of a fascinating nature occur such as finding one's self playing Hamlet stark naked. I suppose the only reason any of us live through opening after opening is that the relief when it's over is so great, even adverse notices can be endured.

The ideal solution would be for a play to open and

get under way by degrees ... allowing the critics to drift in a few each night and staving off the gala crowd until the end of the first week. The actors with more confidence would dish out a far smoother performance and it would all seem less like a Roman Holiday. But the New York first-nighters would be as loath to forego their amusement as the Spaniard to forego bull-fights. So I suppose there's nothing for the actors, authors and managers to do about it except to be lucky enough to be able to give them what they want.

IT'S SUMMER,
BUT IS IT THEATRE?

IT'S SUMMER, BUT IS IT THEATRE?

THE Summer stock company has become a distinctive feature of the American summer scene. There is hardly a vacation district along the Eastern seaboard that hasn't some form of local theatrical enterprise in the way of Community Players, Little Red Barns and Broadways-by-the-Sea. Even west of the Alleghenies and on to the Pacific Coast almost every resort of any comparative size boasts of its repertory theatre. Well, maybe they don't always boast about it, but they have it.

These establishments, like mushrooms, spring up overnight, and a goodly number of them fold up—

also overnight. Some few contrive to keep going with not infrequent changes of management, and an even smaller few thrive and flourish. By the same correlation, a minimum few are excellent, the next few—a large few—are mediocre, and a great many are definitely terrible.

There are far too many people in this world who labor under the El Doradan delusion that the average Summer showhouse is something that can be run with ease, fun and profit. Unfortunately, ours is a land all too favorable for those semi-amateur little aggregations infused with the "goody-goody-let's-give-a-play" spirit who think that all one need do is to get hold of a barn, paint some scenery and put on "Dear Brutus." These are the ones who come under the heading of terrible, and they usually fail rapidly and dismally, and I'm afraid deserve to, if only because their endeavors are apt to turn the local public against the theatre forever.

The mediocre groups are equipped with all good intentions and even talent, but lack of funds make it impossible for them to engage an entire company of first flight actors or to put on any sort of finished performance, and unfortunately, no matter how great may be the merits of a play, the public today is not going to be satisfied with a production in which the cast is competent only in part, and of which the scenery looks as if it had been run up by the village seamstress.

The good, and consequently successful, companies, then, are those well-off, definitely professional play-houses, thoroughly equipped to offer the sort of finished entertainment that can hold its own against the potent opposition of movies, beach parties and dances at the country club. For to run a profitable summer stock company requires more than a converted barn, a bundle of manuscripts and an ambitious crew of players. It requires a locale that is distinctly favorable, and this, I grieve to say, generally implies one that is distinctly wealthy. It costs a lot to operate a theatre. The brief summer season —ten weeks at the most—hardly offers time in which to make up the initial outlay. Without a sold-out subscription list and the sort of patronage that, from motives of local civic pride, can be counted upon in lean years to help make up the deficit, it is hard to keep going. The managements that every week can come across with a finished show, performed by an experienced and professional cast and directed by an expert director, are few indeed.

Just what the contribution of the summer barns is to the American theatre is a matter of divided opinion. I happen to be among those who believe that, generally speaking, they're a good thing, provided, of course, that they belong to the third, or professional, category. To a certain degree, they keep the public theatre-minded. Also, they afford opportunities for trying out new plays—not that the reaction of a summer resort audience is an especially acid test, but it gives the prospective producers a moderately good chance to see what's right or wrong with a script, to decide upon matters of casting and finally to make up their minds whether or not to put on the play the following season.

For actors who might otherwise be wilting forlornly in the offices of Broadway agencies they furnish a job, even at small pay, and an agreeable and healthy way to spend the summer. If an actor is lucky enough to work with a good director and is given parts of reasonable length and variety, a season or two in summer stock is fine experience. It is the nearest approach we now have to the stock company of former halcyon days, and a certain amount of old-fashioned stock work was the finest training in the world.

The experience of playing a new part every week, while it may lead to near-insanity, gives the young player (and even the player not so young) a limbering up, a mastering of quick technique that is invaluable. However, just as newspaper work may be for a time helpful but afterward detrimental to a writer, so too much repertory work may become a bad thing. A new part every week means a frantic struggle to get up in one's lines. There is little or no time for character analysis or any degree of deep study. One tends to depend upon easy tricks which in time may turn into bad mannerisms. But a certain amount of it is of great benefit.

Most of the successful summer playhouses run on the visiting star system. This is a good idea. It attracts the public and helps keep the management out of the red. It also enables the members of the permanent company to come in contact with and maybe learn something from people of importance in the theatre. By people of importance I refer to stars who are stars legitimately and not sporadic products of Hollywood, nor yet those stage-struck authors who, because they've written a best-seller or two, think they can act, and who are about as well equipped for the stage as the average actor is for lecturing on relativity.

Why the people who run summer theatres consider that these interlopers have a drawing value is hard to fathom, unless they go on the theory that the public will come, urged by the same morbid curiosity which lured them at the Century of Progress to hear Mrs. Dionne make a speech. Mrs. Dionne, however, was whisked on and off the platform in five minutes, whereas these lights of the literary firmament carry on for at least two hours. And carry on is right. As an actress who regards the theatre as a profession for which one needs as much training as is required for any highly technical trade, I resent their intrusion, just as I resent another outrage—namely, the occasional appearance of some local débutante with Thespian aspirations and no training who is entrusted with a part because her wealthy mamma is one of the leading patronesses who, when the season is poor, can be counted on to pull the establishment out of the hole.

The summer theatre may approach but it in no way takes the place of the old-time stock company. There is something about even the best of them that doesn't seem quite professional. The average actor is apt to regard a season's experience in one of them as merely a sort of stop-gap for the summer. This may be because it's during the holiday months or because the surroundings are so utterly remote from anything that suggests Broadway.

It's hard to take things too seriously. There's something about arriving at rehearsal and finding one's self face to face with a cast attired in slacks and swimming-shorts that may be colorful, but it's hardly in the tradition of the grand old theatre. The play-houses, too, many of which are perfectly adequate and some few of which are furnished with excellent equipment, have a temporary atmosphere about them—due, doubtless, to the fact that most of them are either fragile, hastily constructed affairs or varia-tions of convertible haylofts. It's an odd sensation to approach a stage door across an open country meadow, and back stage it seems healthy but all wrong somehow to be breathing fresh salt-tinged air instead of the usual dear old dusty dry rot. One feels like anything but a diva making up in a dressing room the size and appearance of a Jones Beach bath-house. Instead of the traditional dust and mouse men-ace, one has to cope with insect life. I for one find it extremely distracting when winged things with hard shells buzz giddily about the stage, sizzle in the footlights, lie kicking on the props or during im-portant scenes crawl menacingly toward one with bloodlust in their eye.

Insects aren't the only creatures attracted by the footlights of the summer theatre. One runs into all manner of pseudo-director, amateur player, would-be designer and the rest of those drama-drunk semi-professionals who can be listed only under the inelegant but expressive title of "phony." On Broadway these people are lost in the more callous and legitimate shuffle. Truth to tell, many of them never get near Broadway at all. One has the impression that during the Winter they hibernate in drama classes of universities or the basements of little theatres and emerge for the summer months. They are usually very enthusiastic and full of technical jargon, and have about them an Olympian air of academic confidence that is quite frightening to the more simple-minded professional. Whatever they have to contribute to the theatre isn't much, and they are, moreover, one of the reasons why these holiday establishments never seem quite genuine theatre.

Then in some places there are students. Some of the summer organizations run a stock company with one hand and a so-called "School of the Theatre" with the other—generally the left. My experience in regard to these is too limited to permit me to speak with any authority, but in some instances I have a nasty suspicion that the school is run less from motives of devotion to the drama than for the purpose of using the pupils' tuition fees for making up the yearly deficit. They do, however, serve their purpose. For the parents of stage-struck girls and boys they solve the problem of how to tide their off-spring over the summer. For those who run the establishments the students come in handy. They can be put to painting scenery and making costumes, which comes under the head of "designing." In plays which call for large casts they can go on as extras, which counts with them as "theatrical experience."

I like students, but they get me down. They have a way of asking questions about acting which are beyond the comprehension of the average simple actor. They waylay one on the way to rehearsal and ask things like, "How do you develop the dynamics of such-and-such a scene?" and they fling about a lot of terms concerning "timing," "shading" and "mood" which are rather terrifying. There are always exceptions, however, and occasionally one encounters some young person with real talent who succeeds in making Broadway and a real part.

Whatever the drawbacks and disadvantages, there can be no doubt that summer stock comes definitely under the heading of fun. That same holiday atmosphere which keeps them from being quite completely professional is part of their charm. To play for a few weeks with the best of them is a delightful and happy experience. As far as the local public is concerned, despite a few voices of dissent from some of the natives and old residents who resent "actor-folk" parading about their beaches and overrunning their tea shoppes, most people welcome a good repertory company in their midst. And, when all's said and done, it all comes under the heading of keeping the theatre going—which in itself is ample reason why these institutions have every right to continue and flourish.